Lincolnshire
COUNTY COUNCIL

discover libraries

This book should be returned on or before the due date.

NBI

11/3

To renew or order library books please telephone 01522 782010
or visit https://lincolnshire.spydus.co.uk
You will require a Personal Identification Number.
Ask any member of staff for this.

The above does not apply to Reader's Group Collection Stock.

Published by AA Publishing (a trading name of AA Media Limited, whose registered office is Fanum House, Basing View, Basingstoke, Hampshire RG21 4EA; registered number 06112600)

© AA Media Limited 2014
First published 2002
Second edition 2008
Third edition 2014

Researched and written by Nick Channer
Field checked and updated 2013 by
Paul Murphy

Mapping in this book is derived from the following products:
OS Landranger 152 (walks 1–4)
OS Landranger 165 (walks 5–16, 18)
OS Landranger 166 (walk 16)
OS Landranger 174 (walks 39–50)
OS Landranger 175 (walks 18–38)
OS Landranger 176 (walks 17, 23, 26)

Contains Ordnance Survey data
© Crown copyright and database right
2014 Ordnance Survey. Licence number
100021153.

A CIP catalogue record for this book is available from the British Library.

ISBNs: 978-0-7495-7565-6
and 978-0-7495-7576-2 (SS)

Series management: David Popey
Editor: Ann F Stonehouse
Designer: Tracey Butler
Proofreader: Karen Kemp
Digital imaging & repro: Ian Little

Cartography provided by the Mapping Services Department of AA Publishing

Printed and bound in the UK by Butler, Tanner & Dennis.

A05099

The Automobile Association would like to thank the following photographers, companies and picture libraries for their assistance in the preparation of this book. Abbreviations for the picture credits are as follows: (t) top; (b) bottom; (l) left; (r) right; (AA) AA World Travel Library.
3 AA/J Tims; 9 AA/M Moody; 10 AA/M Moody; 12/13 AA/M Moody; 23 AA/M Moody; 27 AA/C Jones; 58/59 AA/M Moody; 84/85 AA/V Bates; 101 AA/J Tims; 120/121 AA/M Moody; 134 AA/M Moody; 170 AA/J Tims

Right: Cobstone Windmill, above Turville village (Walk 19)

50 Walks in
BERKSHIRE &
BUCKINGHAMSHIRE

50 Walks of 2–10 Miles

Contents

The walks

Following the walks

An information panel for each walk shows its relative difficulty, the distance and total amount of ascent. An indication of the gradients you will encounter is shown by the rating ▲▲▲ (no steep slopes) to ▲▲▲ (several very steep slopes). Each walk is rated for its relative difficulty compared to the other walks in this book. Walks marked +++ and colour-coded green are likely to be shorter and easier with little total ascent. Those marked with +++ and colour-coded orange are of intermediate difficulty. The hardest walks are marked +++ and colour-coded red.

MAPS

Each walk in this book has a route map. We also suggest an AA or Ordnance Survey map to take with you. The minimum time suggested is for reasonably fit walkers and doesn't allow for stops.

ROUTE MAP LEGEND

- Walk Route
- **1** Route Waypoint
- Adjoining Path
- Viewpoint
- • Place of Interest
- ⌒ Steep Section
- Built-up Area
- Woodland Area
- Toilet
- P Car Park
- Picnic Area
-)(Bridge

START POINTS

The start of each walk is given as a six-figure grid reference prefixed by two letters referring to a 100km square of the National Grid. You'll find more information on grid references on most Ordnance Survey and AA Walker's Maps.

DOGS

We have tried to give dog owners useful advice about how dog friendly each walk is. Please respect other countryside users. Keep your dog under control, especially around livestock, and obey local bylaws and other dog control notices.

CAR PARKING

Many of the car parks suggested are public, but occasionally you may find you have to park on the roadside or in a lay-by. Please be considerate when you leave your car, ensuring that access roads or gates are not blocked and that other vehicles can pass safely.

WALKS LOCATOR

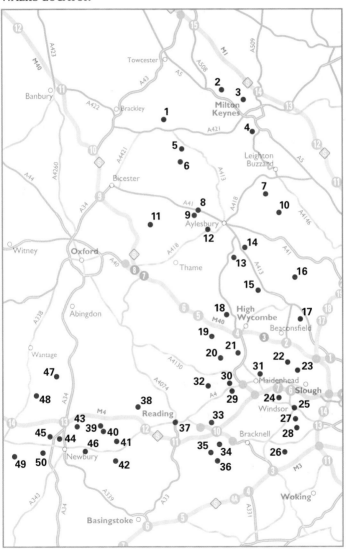

Walking in Berkshire and Buckinghamshire

The adjoining counties of Berkshire and Buckinghamshire have long been recognised as two of England's prettiest shires. Classically English in their beauty and character, they reflect the best of our countryside. Their delightful mix of beech woodland, rolling farmland, quiet waterways and breezy downland conspires to represent some of the finest walking country in Britain. As with other counties in southern England, Berkshire and Buckinghamshire are blessed with many miles of public rights of way, and the routes chosen for this guide reach deep into their rural heartlands, taking advantage of a rich legacy of historic sites and fascinating landmarks.

BUCKINGHAMSHIRE

Buckinghamshire is the larger of the two counties – its shape is often compared to a lion rampant. This is a land of glorious beech trees, wide views and imposing country houses. The Victorian prime minister Benjamin Disraeli, who held office twice, savoured the peace and tranquillity of Hughenden Manor, while generations of statesmen have entertained politicians and world leaders at Chequers, the Prime Minister's rural retreat. Stowe and Waddesdon Manor are fine examples of even grander houses, set amid sumptuous gardens and dignified, orderly parkland.

The Vale of Aylesbury is a vast playground with around 1,000 miles (1,609km) of paths and tracks to explore. Rising above it like protective guardians are the Chiltern Hills, a designated Area of Outstanding Natural Beauty covering 308sq miles (798sq km). They are best appreciated in autumn, when the leaves of the beech trees turn from dark green to deep brown. In the southeast corner of the Chilterns lie the woodland rides of Burnham Beeches, another haven for ramblers, wildlife lovers and those seeking peaceful recreation away from the noise and bustle of the city.

Buckinghamshire's history is long and eventful, but the county is also associated with events within living memory. At Bletchley Park, some 70 years ago, more than 10,000 people worked in complete secrecy to try and bring a swift conclusion to World War II. Further south, an otherwise unremarkable stretch of railway line was made infamous by the Great Train Robbery in the summer of 1963.

BERKSHIRE

Berkshire, too, has much to attract walkers. The county essentially consists of two distinct parts. The western half is predominantly rural, with the Lambourn Downs spilling down to the River Lambourn and the

Right: Heathland near Wokingham (Walk 34)

Berkshire Downs to the majestic Thames. The eastern half of Berkshire may be more urban but here, too, there is the opportunity to get out and savour open spaces. Windsor Great Park and Maidenhead Thicket are prime examples.

Threading their way through the county are two of the South's prettiest rivers – the Lambourn and the Pang. Beyond the tranquil tow paths of the Kennet and Avon Canal, Greenham Common's famous airbase has been transformed to delight walkers.

EXPLORING

Towns and cities are also a feature of this book. The sleepy backwaters of Reading provide a fascinating insight into how the town developed, while a tour of Milton Keynes demonstrates a bold step in city planning.

Each route offers a specific theme to enhance the walk, as well as snippets of useful information on what to look for and what to do while you're there. Most are circular, though some require a train to return to the start. Enjoy the walks and savour the delights of Berkshire and Buckinghamshire's countryside.

PUBLIC TRANSPORT Berkshire and Buckinghamshire are well served by public transport, making many of the walks in this guide easily accessible. For information about local bus services contact Traveline on 0871 200 2233 or consult www.traveline.info. For times of trains consult www.nationalrail.co.uk, or ring 08457 48 49 50.

Above: The Boer War memorial on Coombe Hill (Walks 13 and 14)

Walking in safety

All these walks are suitable for any reasonably fit person, but less experienced walkers should try the easier walks first. Route finding is usually straightforward, but you will find that an Ordnance Survey or AA walking map is a useful addition to the route maps and descriptions; recommendations can be found in the information panels.

RISKS

Although each walk here has been researched with a view to minimising the risks to the walkers who follow its route, no walk in the countryside can be considered to be completely free from risk. Walking in the outdoors will always require a degree of common sense and judgement to ensure that it is as safe as possible.

- Be particularly careful on cliff paths and in upland terrain, where the consequences of a slip can be very serious.
- Remember to check tidal conditions before walking on the seashore.
- Some sections of route are by, or cross, busy roads. Take care and remember traffic is a danger even on minor country lanes.
- Be careful around farmyard machinery and livestock, especially if you have children with you.
- Be aware of the consequences of changes in the weather and check the forecast before you set out. Carry spare clothing and a torch if you are walking in the winter months. Remember the weather can change very quickly at any time of the year, and in moorland and heathland areas, mist and fog can make route finding much harder. Don't set out in these conditions unless you are confident of your navigation skills in poor visibility. In summer remember to take account of the heat and sun; wear a hat and carry water.
- On walks away from centres of population you should carry a whistle and survival bag. If you do have an accident requiring the emergency services, make a note of your position as accurately as possible and dial 999.

COUNTRYSIDE CODE

- Be safe, plan ahead and follow any signs.
- Leave gates and property as you find them.
- Protect plants and animals and take your litter home.
- Keep dogs under close control.
- Consider other people.

For more information visit www.naturalengland.org.uk/ourwork/enjoying/countrysidecode

Overleaf: The River Pang at Pangbourne (Walk 38)

Exploring Stowe Park

DISTANCE 4.5 miles (7.2km)	MINIMUM TIME 2hrs	

ASCENT/GRADIENT Negligible ▲▲▲   LEVEL OF DIFFICULTY ✚✚✚

PATHS Field paths, estate drives, stretches of road; several stiles

LANDSCAPE Farmland and parkland

SUGGESTED MAP OS Explorer 192 Buckingham & Milton Keynes

START/FINISH Grid reference: SP684357

DOG FRIENDLINESS Under control across farmland, on lead within Stowe Park

PARKING On-street parking in Chackmore

PUBLIC TOILETS Stowe Landscape Garden

Stowe has been described as England's greatest work of art and possibly the world's most bewitching landscape garden. But how did it all begin? It was Sir Richard Temple (1634–97), one of Marlborough's generals and described as 'the greatest Whig in the army', who first built a brick mansion here. Work eventually came to an end in 1839 when Stowe's then owner, the 2nd Duke of Buckingham, a descendant of Lord Cobham, suffered financial problems and was declared bankrupt.

Temple's son (1669–1749, also Sir Richard) married a wealthy brewery heiress, became Lord, and later Viscount Cobham and began to extend the house and park. He prided himself on his reputation as a great radical – anti-Stuart and pro-liberty, greatly endorsing the ideals of the Glorious Revolution. Work on the gardens at Stowe started in 1711, but it wasn't until Lord Cobham fell out with George II and his Prime Minister, Robert Walpole, that the idea of an experiment in 'moral gardening' really seized him. Cobham threw himself wholeheartedly into the project. His aim was to create a garden of ideas; a place symbolising the notion of liberty.

MANY HANDS

In 1713 Stowe employed only half a dozen garden staff, but five years later there were almost 30 gardeners. Work at Stowe became a way of life, and so anxious was Cobham for the momentum not to be broken that when his head gardener Edward Bissell broke his leg, he called for a specially adapted chair so that Bissell could continue to work.

In total, Cobham designed eight lakes, constructed more than three dozen temples, and commissioned 50 statues and 40 busts. The country's finest artists and designers, including James Gibbs, William Kent and Sir John Vanbrugh, were employed to help create what the poet James Thomson described as 'the fair majestic paradise of Stowe'. Even Lancelot 'Capability' Brown had a hand in it, beginning his career here in 1741.

Lord Cobham's successors consolidated his work by improving and adding to the garden. However, by the mid-19th century the family fortunes had ebbed away and the estate was sold. After a further sale in 1921, Cobham's vision of an earthly paradise, described by Alexander Pope as 'a work to wonder at', was left virtually empty. The house became a school and the National Trust acquired the garden in 1989.

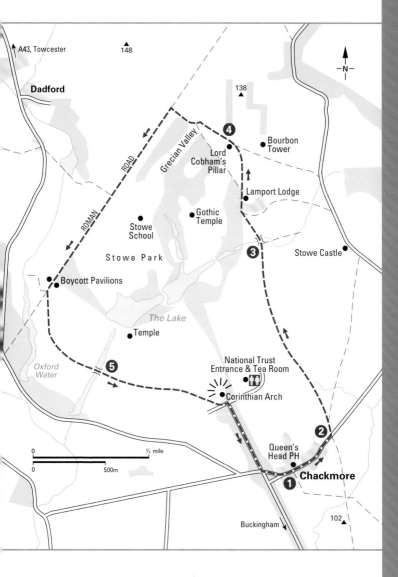

❶ Walk through Chackmore, pass the Queen's Head pub and continue through the village. At the speed de-restriction signs, keep ahead for a few paces and look for a path on the left. Aim diagonally right in the field, passing under power lines. Make for a stile and waymarker beneath the branches of an oak tree in the corner.

❷ Cross the field straight ahead, towards a gate and stile, beyond which is a plank bridge. Keep skirting the boundary of the field to the right all the way to the top far corner. Look left to see the Corinthian Arch at Stowe Park. Go through a kissing gate beside a galvanised gate and join a path. To the right is a fine view of Stowe Castle. Pass under telegraph wires and look for a gap and waymarker ahead. Walk on and cross a footbridge over water. Cross the next field.

❸ At the bottom of the field cross a bridge over a stream and through a gate go into the field and head up the slope, keeping to the left of a house up above. As you climb the slope, the Gothic Temple can be seen to the left. Pass the former Lamport Lodge house, by grand (disused) gates, go through a galvanised gate and continue ahead. The Bourbon Tower is clearly visible over to the right. To the left is Lord Cobham's Pillar. Pass over a stile and continue ahead towards a distant obelisk commemorating the Duke of Buckingham. Merge with another path and keep a sports ground on your right.

❹ Make for a gate leading out to the left of an avenue of trees running down towards the Grecian Valley (only Stowe ticket holders may enter this area). Cross over and follow the track on the right-hand side of the ha-ha up to a clump of trees. Bear left here and follow the wide, straight metalled road, part of a Roman road. Pass the magnificent facade of Stowe School and keep along the main drive. On reaching the Boycott Pavilions, branch off half left along a track to a stile by a cattle grid and a sign for the Corinthian Arch. Down below lies the Oxford Water, crossed by a splendid 18th-century stone bridge.

❺ Follow the drive through the parkland with glimpses of temples and classical designs. The drive eventually reaches the Corinthian Arch. Line up with the arch and pause here to absorb the breathtaking view of Stowe School, surely one of Britain's stateliest vistas. Walk down the avenue to the road junction, swing left and return to Chackmore.

WHERE TO EAT AND DRINK The Queen's Head in Chackmore offers a range of traditional beers and a choice of meals and snacks. There is also a beer garden. An attractive licensed cafe at Stowe serves snacks, lunches and afternoon teas.

WHAT TO SEE The triangular Gothic Temple, used by the Landmark Trust as a holiday let, can be seen from the walk, as can Stowe Castle, a remarkable eye-catcher built in the 18th century. Look out, too, for the Bourbon Tower, which was built in the 1740s as a gamekeeper's lodge in iron-rich Northamptonshire limestone, and given an octagonal turret in 1845.

WHILE YOU'RE THERE The walk skirts the garden, offering good views of some of its classical features, but Stowe offers much more than this and deserves at least a half-day visit in its own right. Plan your walk for the morning so that if what you see whets your appetite, you can pay to enter the grounds in the afternoon and see the whole park.

Around Ouse Valley Park

DISTANCE 2.75 miles (4.4km)   MINIMUM TIME 1hr 15min

ASCENT/GRADIENT Negligible ▲▲▲   LEVEL OF DIFFICULTY ✦✦✦

PATHS Paved walkways, field paths and tow path

LANDSCAPE Fields, canal and river banks, floodplain meadow

SUGGESTED MAP OS Explorer 192 Milton Keynes & Buckingham

START/FINISH Grid reference: SP808415

DOG FRIENDLINESS Lead required in new floodplain forest area

PARKING Small car park next to start of walk, and restricted street parking close by

PUBLIC TOILETS None on route

Barge traffic played an important part in Wolverton's development with loading and unloading from the Grand Union Canal at Galleon Wharf. The Wharf pub was built early in the 19th century to serve canal traffic, and is still here, having changed its name to The Galleon. The canal, Britain's longest man-made waterway at 137 miles (220km), linking London to Birmingham, originally crossed the River Great Ouse near Wolverton by descending almost 33ft (10m) down to the river via nine locks. This was time-consuming at the best of times and in flood conditions often impassable. The solution was an aqueduct. The first brick-built structure, however, collapsed in 1808.

In 1809 canal engineer Benjamin Beavan took up the challenge using the new material of the day – cast iron. His structure featured two cast-iron trough spans which support the massive weight of the water, with a single central masonry pier. The trough is 15ft (4.6m) wide and 6ft 6in (1.98m) deep, with a total length of 101ft (31m). It soon became known as the 'Iron Trunk'. When opened it charged a toll and generated an income of £400 a month (equivalent to £13,500 in today's money) by charging for the extra amount of cargo the canal was able to carry.

In 2011 the Iron Trunk Aqueduct celebrated its bicentenary with a programme of improvement works, including refurbishing the aqueduct and restoring it to its original colours. Today it is still one of the most striking features along the whole stretch of the Grand Union Canal.

Commercial transport on the Grand Union Canal continued to bring prosperity to the area, but by the 1840s canal trade was becoming secondary to the railroad.

THE ADVENT OF THE RAILWAYS

Fortunately, in 1836 Wolverton was chosen as the site of the main locomotive repair shop of the London and Birmingham Railway company (L&BR), serving the line then under construction. The L&BR was one of the first intercity lines in England, and opened in 1838. That same year the impressive Wolverton Viaduct was built. It is 49ft (15m) high and its six major arches span 59ft (18m) each. It was one of the major feats of the L&BR and, in its day, just as impressive as the Iron Trunk. It was widened in 1881.

The Wolverton workshops remained in use until the 1980s – indeed the most recent Royal Train was fitted out at Wolverton in 1977. Today just a few parts of the original works are active, maintaining and repairing rolling stock under the banner of Railcare.

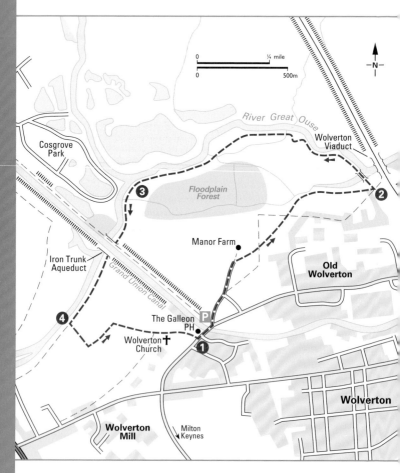

1 With The Galleon at your back turn left, cross the bridge, go past the small car park and take the waymarked path onto a paved track heading to the right, across open fields, with allotments to your right. As you approach Manor Farm house,

veer right and look for a small blue-green gate. Go through it and follow a tree-lined path. The path continues ahead, leaving the trees, and joins a tributary of the Great Ouse (left). Continue ahead at the double gates, signed 'Plant Crossing'.

2 With the Wolverton Viaduct facing you, turn left across the wooden footbridge following the Ouse Valley/Iron Trunk Aqueduct signs. Continue straight ahead with the River Great Ouse to your right and keep following the path, passing a white footbridge that heads north. The 120-acre (49ha) site area (cordoned off) to your left is former quarry workings, home to an innovative proposal to recreate the lost environment of the area's 'Floodplain Forest'. It is the first project of its kind in the UK, where planning permission has been granted for mineral extraction specifically to create a new area of floodplain forest with new planting. On the other side of the River Great Ouse, to your right, is Cosgrove Park.

3 As the caravans and tents of Cosgrove Park end, the Iron Trunk Aqueduct looms into view and the path crosses back over the tributary of the Great Ouse (in summer this may be dry). Climb the steps beside the Iron Trunk Aqueduct up to the Grand Union Canal, with vertiginous views some 40ft (12m) down to the river below. Go back down the steps and squeeze your way through the 'cattle creeps', originally designed to get livestock – and people – from one side of the canal to the other. Continue along the footpath beside the Great Ouse. Soon after passing beneath the aqueduct are two turnings to the left. Ignore these and continue on for around 400yds (366m), then turn left, away from the river.

4 The path winds to the left, then follows the boundary of the field. At the end of the field turn right through a gap in the trees to continue across the next field towards Wolverton Church. After visiting the church, return to the path by which you entered it, turn right and follow this back to the main road. The Galleon is immediately across the side road, to the left.

WHERE TO EAT AND DRINK The Galleon serves typical pub food in a pleasant waterside setting, with a garden that is very popular in summer. If the sun is shining, arrive early for a table and a car parking space.

WHAT TO SEE The Floodplain Forest provides a rich and fertile habitat for plants and animals. It is already one of the best sites in the region for wading birds and has attracted numerous rare birds on migration. As the area is restored, footpaths and bird hides will be installed and the site is scheduled to be fully operational by 2015.

WHILE YOU'RE THERE Wolverton's Saxon Church of Holy Trinity was rebuilt in 1819 in 'Reformed Anglo-Norman' style, on the mounded site of a Norman motte and bailey. Adjacent is a house dating from 1729, formerly the vicarage. The front door has stonework from the 16th-century manor house which stood near by; it includes a coat of arms and pieces from the earlier church building.

A tour of Milton Keynes

DISTANCE 3.5 miles (5.7km)   MINIMUM TIME 2hrs

ASCENT/GRADIENT Negligible ▲▲▲   LEVEL OF DIFFICULTY ✚✚✚

PATHS Paved walkways, boulevards and park paths

LANDSCAPE City centre and park

SUGGESTED MAP OS Explorer 192 Milton Keynes & Buckingham, or street map from tourist information centre

START/FINISH Grid reference: SP842380

DOG FRIENDLINESS Aside from Campbell Park, probably not most dogs' idea of fun

PARKING Car park at Milton Keynes Station

PUBLIC TOILETS Milton Keynes Station and shopping centres

During the 19th century this area of Buckinghamshire began to expand rapidly, largely due to the dawning of the railway era that brought industrial prosperity to places like Newport Pagnell and Wolverton. The opening of the M1 in 1959 sealed the area's future as the site for a new city, which would be required to meet the demands of the business world and its employees, and to accommodate a quarter of a million people. Its name would be Milton Keynes. Contrary to popular opinion this was not a marketing gimmick, based on the amalgamation of two serious-sounding surnames, but in fact the name of an ancient village already in the area. Some 3 miles (5km) east of the current centre it still exists, now called Milton Keynes Village, and, ironically, it remains relatively untouched by the new city.

MONORAILS AND CONCRETE COWS

Initially it was envisaged that Milton Keynes would consist of high-density settlements connected by monorail to a commercial centre – an innovative move, and a far cry from the old concept of garden suburbs previously favoured by Outer London planners. However the monorail system was eventually shelved in favour of a dispersed network of housing, within a US-style grid pattern of roads.

The city became notorious for its number of traffic roundabouts and its ornamental concrete cows, which over the years have become both loved and hated icons of the city. They were commissioned by the town council to symbolise the fact that the new city of Milton Keynes would feature more open green space than found in traditional cities. Its detractors responded by labelling them concrete cows for a concrete city, where its townsfolk would need such models to know how real cows once looked.

Today, some 40 years after the construction began in earnest the name Milton Keynes is still loaded with misconceptions and prejudices; however, its tree-lined boulevards give it a Continental air, and students of modern architecture will enjoy its office buildings which are in a constant state of flux and ownership.

This walk is best done on a sunny summer Sunday, when not only can you still enjoy all the leisure and shopping facilities of the city, but you can also picnic and perhaps watch cricket in the park. Parking spaces are also much easier to find and a lot cheaper than on weekdays.

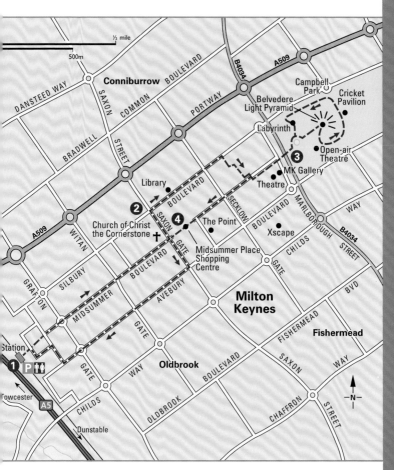

❶ With your back to the railway station, aim slightly left, line up with a row of flagpoles and make for two underpasses. Keep ahead along Midsummer Boulevard, passing the sculpture on the left. Make for the next subway and cross Witan Gate and Upper 5th Street. Go under a third subway, and swing left just before the fourth subway to visit

the domed Church of Christ the Cornerstone. Keep the church on your left and continue to Silbury Boulevard. Ignore the subway to the right and pass under the one straight ahead.

❷ Turn right through a subway and pass Milton Keynes Library. Pass North 9th Street and you will see a pair of letter boxes which were painted gold in 2012, to celebrate the long jump Olympic gold medal of local resident Greg Rutherford. A little further on pass a statue of the Lloyds Bank black horse icon. Swing right and pass under the road to approach the shopping centre at Deer Walk. Don't enter the complex here, but instead turn left and walk along to the next entrance, at Eagle Walk. Go straight through, and emerge at Midsummer Boulevard. Turn left to Field Walk, and turn right here to cross the boulevard. Bear left to reach Milton Keynes Theatre, and adjacent, the MK Gallery, the city's modern art collection. Continue ahead under the subway and cross the footbridge into Campbell Park.

3 Skirt the round pond and make for the 20ft (6m) high 'Light Pyramid' by American artist Liliane Lijn,installed in 2012 on the point known as the Belvedere, with panoramic views over Bedfordshire. Follow the path left down the hill. On the right is the city's open-air theatre. At the circular tree seat continue straight on, signposted

'Cricket Pavilion', and turn left at the totem pole. Continue down the hill, with the cricket pitch and pavilion to your right, and at the next circular tree seat turn left to follow the Art Trail signpost, back towards the city centre. Running parallel to the path are a series of pretty gardens with park benches, which you can divert into and out of at will. Just before you get back to the round pond is the Labyrinth. Retrace your steps back across the bridge, along Midsummer Boulevard, as far as Midsummer Place.

4 Midsummer Place is the city's premier shopping centre with some 50 retailers and an attractive open-air 'square', beneath which stand the original concrete cows, created in 1978 (replicas stand elsewhere in the area). Leave the shopping centre and turn left onto Saxon Gate. Walk along to Avebury Boulevard, glancing left to see Xscape. Turn right to follow the boulevard. Just after crossing Grafton Gate, veer right onto Elder Gate, then left to return to the station.

WHERE TO EAT AND DRINK There are dozens of cafe bars and restaurants in the shopping area in Milton Keynes, mostly of the chain variety. There is also a pleasant cafe in the Church of Christ the Cornerstone.

WHAT TO SEE The Point opened in 1985, to much fanfare, as the UK's first multiplex cinema. It was built in ziggurat form, with red neon lights to connect the apexes at each side so that it looked like a pyramid at night. Alas, with the building now looking tired and outdated, in 2012 plans to demolish it were mooted. The current star of the city skyline is the sleek, metallic, 145ft (44m) wedge-shaped Xscape building, home to the largest real snow ski slope in the UK. It also houses a 16-screen multiplex cinema, two climbing walls, a bowling alley, bars, restaurants and shops. At the Campbell Park end of Xscape a metal book-shaped appendage-like building holds Airkix, where you can skydive indoors in a vertical wind tunnel.

WHILE YOU'RE THERE Visit the Church of Christ the Cornerstone – the first purpose-built ecumenical city-centre church in Britain. The church is 101ft (31m) high, to the top of the lantern, while the cross rises a further 18ft (5.5m), making it the highest point in the city. Surrounding the church is a cloister.

Right: Steel art by Bernard Schottlander, near Christ the Cornerstone Church (Walk 3)

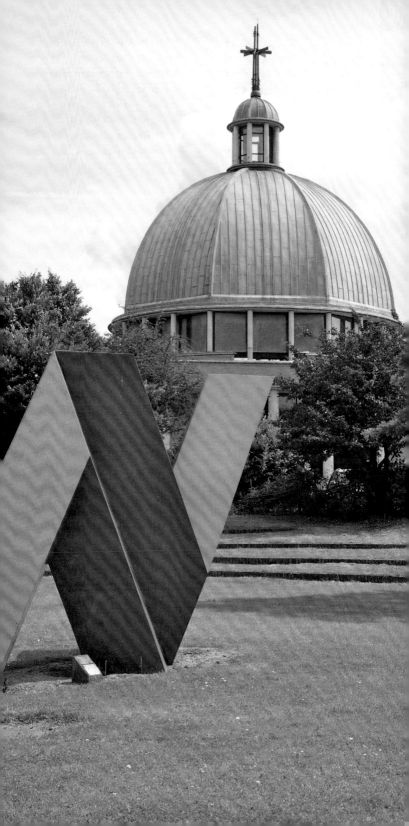

Bletchley Park and Fenny Stratford

DISTANCE 6 miles (9.7km)	MINIMUM TIME 1hr 45min
ASCENT/GRADIENT Negligible ▲ ▲ ▲	LEVEL OF DIFFICULTY + + +

PATHS Roads, park and field paths, canal tow path and riverside walk

LANDSCAPE Mixture of suburban streets and farmland

SUGGESTED MAP OS Explorer 192 Buckingham & Milton Keynes

START/FINISH Grid reference: SP868337

DOG FRIENDLINESS Lead required in Blue Lagoon Park, along Broad Walk and by canal

PARKING Bletchley Station and approach road

PUBLIC TOILETS Bletchley Station and Bletchley Park

The importance of what took place at Bletchley Park during World War II cannot be overstated. This was the home of Station X – where, at its height, some 10,000 people worked in total secrecy in a small, nondescript town at the heart of the English shires to infiltrate the most important secrets of Germany's war machine.

BRAIN TEASERS

Why Bletchley? Midway between the keenest brains of the universities of Oxford and Cambridge, and just a few minutes' walk from a mainline railway station with regular services to London, this country estate seemed a perfect venue for the Government Code and Cypher School. As the threat of war loomed, Bletchley Park geared up to become the key communications centre in the history of modern warfare.

In August 1939, code breakers arrived at Bletchley Park in numbers. So as not to arouse suspicion in the area, they posed as members of 'Captain Ridley's shooting party'. Once here mathematicians, linguists, crossword enthusiasts and Oxbridge boffins plotted ceaselessly – in the main grand house, in wooden huts and in brick-built blocks, many of which still stand today. Their role was to study the German military cipher machine, 'Enigma', and devise a programme to enable the Allies to decode the Nazis' secret messages. The odds against anyone who did not know the settings being able to break Enigma were a staggering 159 million million million to one. But the team at Bletchley Park did break Enigma, and as a result shortened the war against Germany by as much as two years, thus saving countless lives.

The Germans never realised Enigma had been broken, and indeed, until the mid-1970s no one outside Bletchley Park knew exactly what went on here. Today it is the subject of television programmes and films, with a new movie, *The Imitation Game*, scheduled for 2015 starring Benedict Cumberbatch (as Alan Turing, a key player in the real-life drama here) and Keira Knightley.

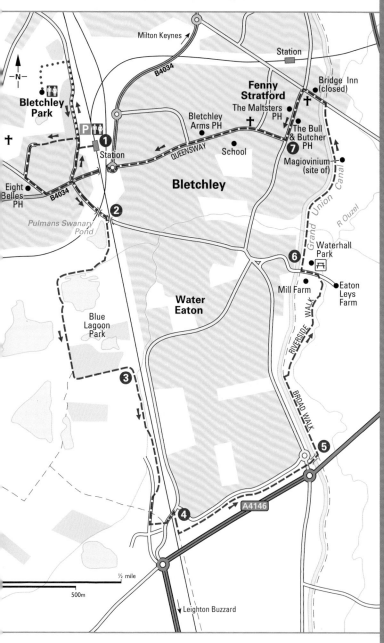

❶ From the station car park cross the road. To visit Bletchley Park, turn right – the entrance is 300yds (274m)

further along Sherwood Drive. Retrace your steps towards the station and turn right onto the footpath opposite.

This brings you into Wilton Avenue. Turn left here, then left into Church Green Road. Bear left at the junction with Buckingham Road. Turn right into Water Eaton Road, go under a high bridge, then bear right at the footpath sign, just before the next bridge.

2 Pass a pond belonging to an Angling Club on the right, and follow the fenced path to a disused stile. Continue to a fork, keep right and follow the track right (anti-clockwise) round the edge of the lake. Go down one set of steps, up and down another, avoid a third set, then as you leave the lake behind, cross the two sets of steps and a footbridge on the right. Turn left immediately beyond and keep green railings to your right. Eventually bear left at a grassy track and follow it to a metal gate and stile. Turn right in front of these. Swing left, then right, and continue straight ahead with the railway line left.

3 Pass through trees, and alongside a waste recycling plant and a building site. Eventually you will have to leave the path as it is blocked by building materials. Walk along the road, bear left, cross the railway bridge and turn immediately right at yellow posts.

4 Follow the path for a short distance, then turn left at a waymarker. Continue, with houses on your left. On

reaching the road, cross it between two roundabouts, cross the canal bridge, and turn left to follow tree-lined Broad Walk, parallel to the tow path.

5 Continue ahead, to fork right at the Riverside Walk sign, then swing left after about 75yds (69m). Fork right to keep following the river. When you are level with Eaton Leys Farm on the right, cross a footbridge over a pond and turn left. Pass Mill Farm (left) and the car park to Waterhall Park (right). Just before the humpback bridge, turn right onto the Grand Union Canal tow path.

6 Continue ahead, and eventually pass a lift bridge and small private marina and leave the tow path. Turn left across the canal bridge, pass the Bridge Inn (now closed), and the Swan Hotel. Turn left into Aylesbury Street, past the church on the corner and walk through Fenny Stratford past The Maltsters and The Bull and Butcher pubs. At the mini-roundabout turn right into Vicarage Road.

7 Continue straight on over a roundabout into Queensway which eventually heads into the main shopping area, pedestrianised Elizabeth Square. Pass to the right of the Brunel Shopping Centre, go left up a ramp, pass beneath the railway line, turn right at the police station into Sherwood Drive and return to the station.

WHERE TO EAT AND DRINK There are many pubs along the route, and towards the end of the walk Queensway offers plenty of places for a coffee. There are picnic tables at Waterhall Park. If you are visiting Bletchley Park, they have a cafe–restaurant and picnic tables.

WHAT TO SEE When the tower of Fenny Stratford Church comes into view as you walk along the canal, look right to the site of the Roman town of Magiovinium. The bank and ditch surrounding it can be identifd in aerial photographs, and the site is protected as a scheduled ancient monument. The enclosed part of Magiovinium straddles Watling Street and once covered about 18.5 acres (7.5ha).

Right: Bletchley Park, the wartime intelligence centre (Walk 4)

From Addington to Metroland

DISTANCE 4.25 miles (6.8km)	MINIMUM TIME 1hr 45min

ASCENT/GRADIENT 88ft (27m) ▲▲▲   LEVEL OF DIFFICULTY ✚✚✚

PATHS Quiet country road, field paths, national trails; many stiles

LANDSCAPE Gently undulating farmland either side of Claydon Brook

SUGGESTED MAP OS Explorer 192 Buckingham & Milton Keynes

START/FINISH Grid reference: SP742285

DOG FRIENDLINESS Lead required on road and near livestock

PARKING Limited space by church in Addington – avoid Sunday morning

PUBLIC TOILETS None on route

Addington is one of Buckinghamshire's remoter settlements, and if you drive into it off the main A413, entering through a set of double gates, you'll wonder if you have in fact strayed onto private property. This is because the village was built very much around Addington Manor, and it still has that almost feudal atmosphere, with many grand elegant central buildings and houses, surrounded by several farms.

The present manor house is a 19th-century building on the site of the much older structure, which was used twice during the English Civil War as the national headquarters of the Parliamentarian forces. During World War II the new house was, for a time, the residence of the Czechoslovak Military Intelligence staff who planned the assassination of the high-ranking Nazi official Reinhard Heydrich (one of the main architects of the Holocaust) from here. Today the manor is famous as an equestrian centre, and was used by Team GB as one of their training venues for the final build up to the London 2012 Olympic Games. There is no public access to the house or grounds.

UNDERGROUND TO OVERGROUND

Near the start of the walk you will pass Verney Junction, a working railway station between 1868 and 1968. It's hard to imagine today, but in 1933 this remote outpost became the terminus of the London Underground's Metropolitan Line, which began more than 50 miles (80km) to the south at London's Baker Street (today leafy suburban Chesham holds the distinction of being the end of the line).

For a brief period Verney Junction was therefore part of 'Metroland' – that dreamy Utopia encompassing a modern home in beautiful countryside with a fast railway service to central London. Metroland was invented by the Metropolitan Railway's shrewd marketing department and popularised by the poetry of John Betjeman. In its heyday seaside excursions as far south as Ramsgate could even be booked from Verney Junction.

The dream lasted just three years, with the Metropolitan link to here closing in 1936. By late 1940 Verney Junction had returned to its humble roots, functioning as a rural interchange for local services. Following the decline in rail freight and rural depopulation (among other factors), it suffered the fate of so many other remote rural stations in the 1960s. The last train ran in 1968, and in the same year the station was demolished.

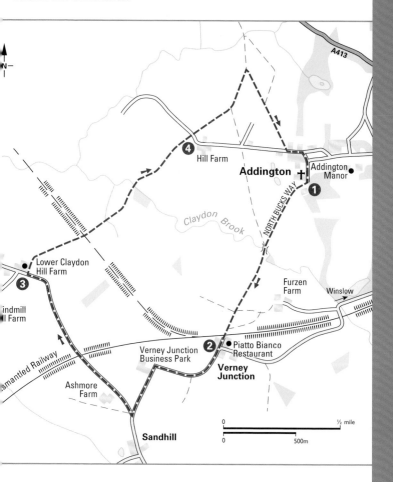

❶ With Addington Church on your right, and a modern house with a well in the front garden on your left, go through the gate and follow the North Buckinghamshire Way across farmland. After 450yds (411m) you come to a stile and narrow footbridge over the Claydon Brook. Continue ahead to a stile and plank bridge and keep to the right edge of the next field. Over to the left lies Furzen Farm. Cross a track and a stile, then make for a kissing gate. Cross this to discover a section of overgrown, long-disused railway line. A 'Stop, Look and Listen' railway sign is still in place.

❷ Follow the North Buckinghamshire Way ahead, keeping The Station House of 1870 on the right. Now a private residence, this was part of Verney Junction Station. Note the Victorian postbox in the wall. Walk along the road to the old Verney Arms pub, which opened in 1890 as The Station Arms and now houses a restaurant. Keep right at the junction. Follow the road passing Verney Junction Business Park, and bear right at the next junction for Buckingham and Padbury. Re-cross the old railway at the next bridge – look over to the left-hand side where some of the old track is still visible – and continue along the road, following it round a left bend. When you see a black metal sign for 'Lower Claydon Hill Farm/Alborada Alpacas' look to turn right to join the Cross Bucks Way.

❸ Cross a stile and bridge and follow the fence along to a second stile. Go diagonally right in the next field, passing under electricity cables, and cross the site of an old railway line (no traces now remain) via two stiles. Go straight ahead in the next field to a galvanised gate and then, through the gate, veer to the left of a stand of trees. Cross back over the Claydon Brook via a stile and a narrow footbridge with a stile at each end. Once safely across here, veer diagonally right. Across the field are two gates; make for the left-hand one and head diagonally up the field, towards the right corner and the farm.

❹ Draw level with Hill Farm, pass through a waymarked gate (climb over it if it is secured), walk a few paces up the track, turn right, cross a stile to another stile, then go half left to reach a track and three stiles. Once over these, aim diagonally right across the field to a stile by a galvanised gate (ignore the stile to the left). Cross over it and go straight ahead into the next field through a gate, then head diagonally right to a corner of the field where you will find a waymarker and stile. Bear left and walk along the lane to a road junction with a one-way traffic arrow. Turn right here, then bear right again at the next junction and return to the church.

WHERE TO EAT AND DRINK The only option on the route is the rather formal Piatto Bianco restaurant, housed in The Verney Arms, which ceased to be a pub some years ago (Point ❷). It offers standard Italian favourites and a reasonably priced two-course lunchtime menu. Neighbouring Winslow has a good choice of pubs, cafes and restaurants.

WHAT TO SEE At the very end of the walk, just before turning back to the church, you will pass the gardens and outbuildings of Addington Manor – look out for the old village stocks, hanging on a wall.

WHILE YOU'RE THERE Addington's secluded church stands at the end of a long drive and is renowned for its windows, which contain the largest collection of Dutch glass in an English church. The roundels date to the 16th and early 17th centuries, and the windows mainly illustrate biblical scenes. The great conductor Sir Malcolm Sargeant (1895–1967) lived in a cottage at Addington during World War II, and sometimes played the church organ here.

Around the Claydons

DISTANCE 5.5 miles (8.8km)   MINIMUM TIME 2hrs

ASCENT/GRADIENT 160ft (49m) ▲▲▲   LEVEL OF DIFFICULTY ✦✦✦

PATHS Field paths and tracks, several stretches of road; several stiles

LANDSCAPE Gentle farmland and parkland in the Vale of Aylesbury

SUGGESTED MAP OS Explorer 192 Buckingham & Milton Keynes

START/FINISH Grid reference: SP739255

DOG FRIENDLINESS Dogs on lead at all times around livestock

PARKING On-street parking in road leading to St Mary the Virgin Church, East Claydon

PUBLIC TOILETS None on route, but Claydon House for visitors

Standing amid elegant parkland, studded with cedar, oak, horse chestnut, holm oak and Wellingtonia trees, 18th-century Claydon House replaced an earlier building and is now in the care of the National Trust. Only one third of the house remains, and on seeing it for the first time you may be struck by its simplicity – yet its interior holds a series of magnificent and distinctive rococo state rooms with carving by Luke Lightfoot. You can also see the bedroom used by Florence Nightingale (1820–1910) during visits to her sister, who lived here.

CLAYDON HOUSE

In 1620 Edmund Verney, Knight-Marshal and Standard Bearer to Charles I, became the first Verney to occupy Claydon. Later, during the 18th century, the family succeeded to an earldom, and Edmund's great-great-grandson, Ralph, 2nd Earl Verney, began to remodel the Tudor manor house, attempting to outdo nearby Stowe. This work still forms the core of the three-storey brick east wing, although the design has disappeared as a result of successive rebuilding.

Ralph also added the stone-faced west wing, employing the services of the unknown Luke Lightfoot, an eccentric and enigmatic figure who had acquired certain skills as a craftsman and was variously described as a cabinetmaker, carver, architect and surveyor. However, there was a darker side to Lightfoot. He was also a swindler, which almost certainly came to light just as his work was nearing completion, for he was dismissed in 1769.

Undeterred, Verney continued with his building plan, though now beset by financial problems. He added a domed entrance hall to the west wing and beyond that a ballroom, but died soon after in 1791, penniless and miserable. His niece, Lady Fermanagh, inherited Claydon and within a year she had demolished her uncle's precious ballroom and entrance hall. The house was bequeathed to the National Trust in 1956.

THE LADY WITH THE LAMP

Florence Nightingale, whose sister married Sir Harry Verney, was a frequent visitor to Claydon between the late 1850s and 1895. She would often spend her summers at the house, and over the fireplace in her bedroom is a portrait of her by W B Richmond. Adjacent to it is a watercolour by Alfred E Chalon depicting Florence with her sister and their mother. A museum displays Verney family mementoes and objects associated with Florence Nightingale and her experiences during the Crimean War.

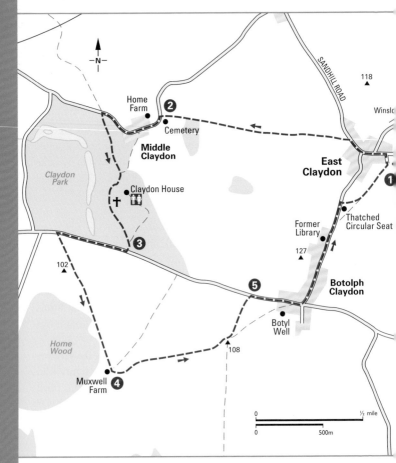

1 Walk along Church Way, past the Winslow road, to the village centre and keep right at the next junction, following Sandhill Road. Pass a row of houses, set back from the road on the right, and swing left just before a brick-and-timber cottage to pass through a kissing gate beside a galvanised gate. Go straight ahead towards a wooden gate and waymarker. Go through it and continue ahead in the field, with the boundary on your right. Make for a gate in the corner and cross the next large field, straight ahead through the middle of it, making for a clump of trees. Veer to the right of the trees and continue ahead with the hedgerow on the left. Turn left onto the road, with Home Farm directly opposite and a cemetery to your left.

❷ Follow the road for 600yds (549m), passing the entrance to Home Farm on the right and a footpath on the left. Go round two bends, then turn left and follow the drive to Claydon House. Nearing the house, bear right at a waymarker post, go right through a gate right by the house, then turn left alongside the house and its ha-ha. Keep the house and the church on your left and continue, with its lakes and parkland over to your right. Cut straight ahead through the park to reach a gate, merge with the drive to Claydon House and follow it out to the road.

❸ Turn right and pass a lay-by. Continue along the roadside until you reach a stile in the left boundary. Head diagonally left across a large field, towards a hedge corner, and then, maintaining the same direction, make for the extreme left corner of Home Wood. Cross a stile into the next field. Veer half left, with the woodland edge on your right, passing left of a small pond to a gap in the hedge with a waymarker post and a plank bridge. Make for a gate and stile ahead and cross a tarmac drive to Muxwell Farm.

❹ Beyond a gate, head diagonally left and look for a waymarker in the line of trees across the pasture. Veer right in the next field, making for a stile and post in the boundary. Walk diagonally right across the field to the far corner, pass through a gap and keep to the right edge of the pasture. Bear right at a gateway to a track and turn left. Walk along to the road and turn right.

❺ Walk through picture-postcard Botolph Claydon and bear left at the junction, following the signs for East Claydon and Winslow. Pass Botolph Farmhouse, the village library and hall, a clocktower and an unusual thatched circular seat built round a tree. Around 50 paces beyond the latter follow the pavement right towards a playground. This path leads back to the church at East Claydon.

WHERE TO EAT AND DRINK There are a separate restaurant and tea rooms at Claydon House, serving high-quality refreshments in attractive historic settings. There are no pubs on the route of the walk, but nearby Winslow is a busy and attractive centre with a good choice of pubs, cafes and restaurants.

WHAT TO SEE St Mary the Virgin Church at East Claydon dates back to the 13th century, and the tower was built in the late 15th century. Look out for the former library at Botolph Claydon, built in 1900, and now the village hall. Beside it stands a clock tower erected in 1913, dedicated to Sir Edmund Verney in remembrance of his work for the welfare of the parish.

WHILE YOU'RE THERE If time and energy allow, leave the route of the walk near Claydon House and explore the local countryside, parkland and walks round the lakes on 'permissive paths' (where use by the public is allowed by the landowner) to the west of the house.

Mentmore and the Grand Union Canal

DISTANCE 6.5 miles (10.4km)	MINIMUM TIME 2hrs 45min	
ASCENT/GRADIENT 180ft (55m) ▲▲▲	LEVEL OF DIFFICULTY ✦✦✦	

PATHS Field paths and tracks, roads and canal tow path; several stiles

LANDSCAPE Vale of Aylesbury and farmland west of Grand Union Canal

SUGGESTED MAP AA Walker's Map 24 The Chilterns

START/FINISH Grid reference: SP907196

DOG FRIENDLINESS On lead across farmland and under control on tow path

PARKING Limited parking in vicinity of The Stag pub at Mentmore

PUBLIC TOILETS None on route

It hardly seems possible today, but in the summer of 1963, 15 masked men waited in the darkness of the Buckinghamshire countryside, held up the night train from Glasgow to London and robbed it of £2.5 million. It was described as 'the Great Train Robbery' and the crime of the century, making newspaper headlines around the world and eventually turning the thieves into folk heroes, immortalised in books, television series and money-spinning movies. The criminals were pursued and captured by Scotland Yard and many of them were given long prison sentences. But the story did not end there as one of them, Ronald Biggs, broke out of jail, fled to Brazil and eluded capture for the next 35 years.

THE GREAT TRAIN ROBBERY

These days, surplus and used bank notes are transported around the country in security vans, but in the very different world of the early 1960s, express trains conveyed such consignments – often with huge amounts of money on board. And 50 years ago it was possible to stop a mail train and rob it – as was proved.

The men planned the snatch in meticulous detail, surveying the railway line between London and Rugby to find an isolated stretch of track with a signal and easy access to the road. Eventually they found what they were looking for – Sears Crossing and nearby Bridego Bridge on the Buckinghamshire/Bedfordshire border, to the south of Leighton Buzzard. They made many trips here in the dead of night, to identify the mail trains and plan the job. Satisfied that it could be done, their next step was to familiarise themselves with the technicalities of train engines and braking systems. To do this, they dressed up in navy blue boiler suits, passing themselves off as railway workers in the marshalling yards of London's mainline stations.

In the early hours of Thursday 8 August, 1963, the men were as ready as they ever would be. It was time to go. Travelling in a convoy of vehicles, they made their way across country to the four-track railway. Their first task was to cut the telephone wires to the nearby farms. Then, as the mail train approached, they covered the green light with a glove and used a battery and a bulb behind the red signal to give the impression to the driver that the light was against him. The train stopped, but the driver refused to co-operate and received violent blows to the head. With the engine and the vital Post Office coaches detached from the rest of the train, the robbers moved the express down the line to Bridego Bridge where they unloaded 120 sacks onto the vehicles lined up on the road below. They drove off as dawn gradually lit the scene of their extraordinary crime (see also Walk 11).

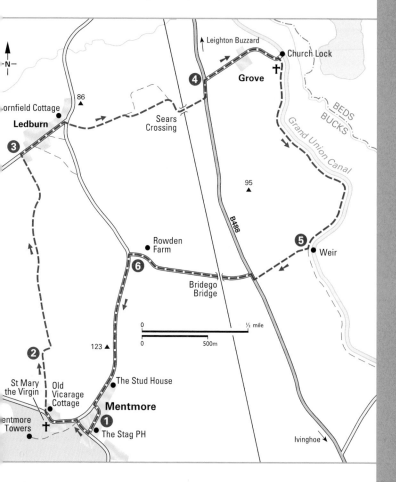

❶ Walk back to the junction by The Stag pub, turn right and shortly pass one of the grand entrances to Mentmore Towers. Follow the road round to the left, then to the right by the Church of St Mary the Virgin. Continue along the road and turn right at a stile, just beyond Old

Vicarage Cottage. Go down the field, keeping the fence over to the right, and look for a stile in the bottom boundary to the left of a solitary oak and farm sheds.

2 Over the stile veer right for 50 paces to a plank bridge, then turn left to skirt the field, keeping a ditch on the left. On reaching the next plank bridge and waymarker, look for a pond enclosed by fencing. Follow the path alongside it and then through a young copse into the next field. Pass under telegraph wires to the next plank bridge in the boundary. Go ahead into a large field and pass under electricity cables. The houses of Ledburn can be seen ahead. Make for a footbridge and in the next field, where the ditch veers sharply right, go ahead and aim slightly left, towards a house with a white-painted gable. Keep to the left of it and turn right at the road.

3 Go through Ledburn and make for a left bend. On the left is Cornfield Cottage, once a chapel. Cross the road to a kissing gate and follow a track running across farmland. After a while look for a waymarker post on a left bend, and keep ahead, following the path across the middle of a field. At a track, turn right and follow it to Sears Crossing, bearing to the left

of a clump of trees to regain the overgrown path. Cross the railway bridge, follow the track down to the road and turn left.

4 Bear right at the sign for Grove Church and Farm and walk down to the Grand Union Canal at Church Lock. Pass Church Lock Cottage before turning right to join the tow path. Follow it for about 1 mile (1.6km), and 140yds (128m) before a bridge, where you can see a weir topped by planks on the left, leave the tow path at a plank bridge and bear right for 40 paces to the field corner.

5 Swing left and keep the boundary on your right. Make for the road and exit via two metal gates. Turn right, then left at the turning for Wing and Ledburn. Follow the road to Bridego Bridge, pass beneath the railway and keep ahead to eventually pass Rowden Farm.

6 Bear left at the T-junction for Mentmore. Pass Mentmore Courts, Howell Hill Close and The Stud House before turning left at the end of a stretch of pavement. Opposite the junction are two wooden gates leading into a field. Follow the road round to the right and return to the playground and parking area.

WHERE TO EAT AND DRINK The Stag at Mentmore was closed at the time of checking (summer 2013). A buyer for this famous old pub is anticipated, but do check ahead if you are visiting. At neighbouring Cheddington, try the upmarket sandwiches and gastropub menu at The Old Swan.

WHAT TO SEE The former Church of St Michael and All Angels by Church Lock was once the smallest church in the county, and is mentioned in the Domesday Book. The church was rebuilt during the 14th century and declared redundant in 1971. It is now a private house.

WHILE YOU'RE THERE Have a look at the Church of St Mary the Virgin at Mentmore. Make for the wooded corner of the churchyard and you'll glimpse splendid Mentmore Towers, once the home of Lord Rosebery, a Liberal Prime Minister in the latter years of the 19th century.

From Quainton to Waddesdon

DISTANCE 5 miles (8km)   MINIMUM TIME 2hrs

ASCENT/GRADIENT Negligible ▲▲▲   LEVEL OF DIFFICULTY ✚✚✚

PATHS Mainly field paths, some stretches of road, parts of North Buckinghamshire Way and Midshires Way; many stiles

LANDSCAPE Gentle farmland in Vale of Aylesbury

SUGGESTED MAP OS Explorer 181 Chiltern Hills North

START/FINISH Grid reference: SP736189

DOG FRIENDLINESS Mostly on lead, particularly near farm buildings

PARKING Buckinghamshire Railway Centre car park (permission given)

PUBLIC TOILETS Buckinghamshire Railway Centre (with permission)

The Buckinghamshire Railway Centre at Quainton Road Station is one of those wonderful, largely unheralded types of place where – if you've the spirit and the imagination – you can wallow for hours in nostalgia, reliving the days when Britain could be proud of its railway system.

THE BUCKINGHAMSHIRE RAILWAY CENTRE

Covering 25 acres (10ha), the site is like a miniature version of York's famous National Railway Museum, hosting one of the country's largest independent collections of railway engines and rolling stock, and offering vintage steam train rides and half-day steam locomotive driving courses among its attractions. The centerpiece is the glass-roofed Victorian station, which houses a flower-filled platform with nostalgic adverts, and some star engines and rolling stock used by VIPs. In fact this part of the centre is the old Oxford Rewley Road railway station, a listed building (constructed 1888), which was moved piece by piece from Oxford in 2001 and rebuilt here. More leviathans of the railway age are to be seen outside, while others are being restored in the sheds.

Opened in 1868 as part of the Aylesbury and Buckingham Railway, Quainton Road Station was absorbed by the Metropolitan Railway in 1890, becoming one of those far-flung rural stations you tend to associate with the best of Ealing comedy films. In those days you could change at Quainton Road for the Metropolitan Line and travel all the way to Baker Street. Look out for the station sign on the original Quainton Road Station platform (outside) advising passengers to change here for the Metropolitan Line. By the turn of the 19th century, it was also possible to travel from here direct to London's Marylebone or north to Manchester.

As time went on, Quainton became the meeting point of three railways – the Metropolitan Railway, the Brill Tramway and the London extension of the Great Central Railway. As rail lost popularity to roads, the relative isolation of Quainton meant that these lines were no longer viable.

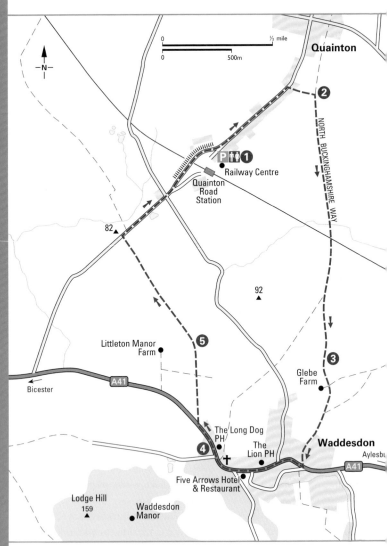

❶ Turn right from the car park and follow Station Road towards Quainton. Pass the houses, and when the road curves left, turn right at a footpath sign and stile to follow a track between fields. Quainton and its windmill can be seen on the left.

Go through a gateway and turn immediately right to join the North Buckinghamshire Way.

❷ Follow the edge of the field to a kissing gate by a field gate, and continue to a stile in the distant boundary. Cross the stile and continue ahead. Pass through a steel gate and stile. Continue ahead across the field, veering slightly left. Here you'll find a stile, footbridge and two more stiles all next to each other. Cross the next small field, then a stile, then cross the railway line. Go over a plank bridge, a stile, then two stiles (the second a squeeze stile) through a hedge. Continue beside the hedge, right, for the length of the next long rectangular field, making for telegraph poles. Go over a stile, by the poles and a metal crash barrier, and continue straight ahead on a concrete track. Waddesdon Manor's pinnacled skyline may be glimpsed up in the trees, right of the church. When the track bends right, go through a kissing gate into the field and turn immediately right.

❸ Skirt Glebe Farm and cross a track via two kissing gates. At the second of the two, aim diagonally right to two stiles and continue alongside a hedgerow, left, in the next field. Go through a kissing gate, cross the field, keeping left, then through another kissing gate to join an enclosed path running into Waddesdon. Turn right onto the main street, past The Lion pub. Across the road note the ornate Five Arrows Hotel and Restaurant

building. Continue and enter the church gate on the right. Leave the churchyard by the side gate, coming back onto the road alongside The Long Dog pub.

❹ Follow the road out of the village, passing an old cast-iron milepost. Around 50 paces beyond the speed de-restriction sign, turn right at a waymarker through a kissing gate. Go through a second kissing gate and continue straight ahead across the next field. Cross a concrete farm track, and continue straight ahead, passing under power lines. Aim for a kissing gate and footbridge in the boundary hedge, but beware that the approach to this may be completely overgrown and you will have to come at it from the left-hand side.

❺ Aim slightly left in the next field to reach a kissing gate, and then go diagonally left across the next pasture to a kissing gate in the far corner. Continue along the left of the hedge and make for a kissing gate by a field gate. After a few paces go through another kissing gate, turn right and follow the road. From the bridge there is a good view of the railway centre. Go over it and return to the car park.

WHERE TO EAT AND DRINK There are refreshments at the Railway Centre, but for high-quality cooking try Waddesdon. The Lion does typical pub food, while The Long Dog has a more varied menu, including tapas.

WHAT TO SEE Picturesque Quainton Windmill, clearly visible at the start of the walk, was built between 1830 and 1832. It is a 65ft (20m), six-storey brick tower mill, and is Buckinghamshire's tallest windmill. It stopped working in the 1890s, fell derelict and was not rescued until 1974. Now partially restored, it can once again grind wheat into flour. It is open to visitors on Sundays (10am to 1pm).

WHILE YOU'RE THERE Do make time to see the Railway Centre. Although at first sight it may seem to be geared towards railway enthusiast and children, it offers much wider historical and visual interest. Simply standing beneath the giant black South African steam train, outside in the yard, and imagining it thundering across the Veldt is an experience in itself.

Waddesdon Manor and Waddesdon

DISTANCE 3 miles (4.8km)	MINIMUM TIME 1hr 15min

ASCENT/GRADIENT 250ft (76m) ▲▲▲   LEVEL OF DIFFICULTY ✦✦✦

PATHS Mostly parkland and drives, some fields and gravel track

LANDSCAPE Formal country park and woodland

SUGGESTED MAP OS Explorer 181 Chiltern Hills North

START/FINISH Grid reference: SP741169

DOG FRIENDLINESS Mostly on lead, particularly near farm buildings; not allowed in grounds of Waddesdon Manor

PARKING On Baker Street, off Waddesdon High Street (A41)

PUBLIC TOILETS None on route

The story of the Rothschilds can be traced back to Frankfurt's Jewish ghetto in the 16th century. Mayer Amschel Rothschild founded the famous banking dynasty in the 18th century, and by the 19th century they had became the richest and one of the most powerful families in Europe, acting as bankers to monarchs and governments. They built palaces and castles, and collected fine and decorative art.

Baron Ferdinand de Rothschild (1839–98) bought the Waddesdon Estate – then nothing but farmland – and had French architect Gabriel-Hippolyte Destailleur build him a country retreat in the style of a Loire château. It was created as a place to entertain guests, most famously at the baron's weekend house parties which included figures from the social circle around the Prince of Wales.

THE ROTHSCHILD DYNASTY

Several of the houses, now outside the estate in Waddesdon itself, and including the village hall, were rebuilt by Ferdinand de Rothschild. They can be distinguished by maroon-painted gables and ornate architectural detail, and all feature the same Rothschild family symbol: five arrows held in a fist on a red shield. The red shield is a reminder of the house, Zum Roten Schild ('At the sign of the red shield'), which the family's 16th-century forefathers had inhabited in Frankfurt. This is also where the Rothschild name comes from. The five arrows represent Mayer Amschel's five sons, four of whom established banking houses in Europe's leading financial centres of the day – London, Vienna, Naples and Paris. The fist symbolises their close links: the branches of the family are descended from the five brothers and to keep even closer links they often intermarried cousins, though this practice ceased in the 19th century.

As a family, the Rothschilds were also among the greatest collectors of the 19th century, seeking the highest quality of workmanship and always with a keen sense of historical importance. The houses that they built, the interiors they created and the magnificent collections within them became known internationally as the 'goût Rothschild' referring to a detailed, elaborate style of interior decoration and living which had its origins in 19th-century France, Britain and Germany. Waddesdon is one of the rare survivors of that splendour.

Waddesdon Manor passed through the dynasty until the late 1950s. By this time the heyday of the grand country house was long gone, and without an heir, James de Rothschild and his wife, Dorothy, decided to leave the house, its nationally important collections of paintings and porcelain, and 165 acres (67ha) of garden and park to The National Trust. The family is still very much involved in the Manor, with the estate administered by a Rothschild charitable trust, overseen by Baron Jacob Rothschild (b. 1936), a British investment banker. This continues a long-standing and distinguished family philanthropic tradition, as underlined by the Rothschild Foundation on Windmill Hill.

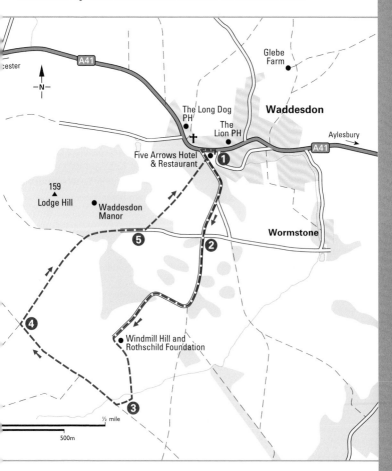

1 From Baker Street go back up to the High Street, turn left, go immediately left past The Five Arrows, and turn left onto Silk Street for the public entrance to Waddesdon Manor. Pass through the ornate gates and follow the drive through trees. Where it veers left, by a waymarker, go straight on along a grass track to a T-junction, passing first a bowling green, then a cricket ground on your right.

2 Go straight uphill, past the sign for Windmill Hill Farm. Continue on the bridleway as it bends right and left, crossing two cattle grids. At a sign for Windmill Hill, The Rothschild Foundation and Windmill Hill Cottage bear left and follow the track, passing a pair of cottages on the left. Keep left at the modern Rothschild Foundation buildings and descend the steep slope to the bottom. As it flattens out, go into the field, crossing the ditch, and turn immediately right.

3 In the corner of the field cross back over the ditch by the bridleway marker. Go through two field gates straight ahead up the hill, keeping to the right of the field. Go though

another gate onto a stony track and continue ahead.

4 At the next public bridleway sign turn right through a kissing gate and over a plank bridge, and walk straight ahead towards Waddesdon Manor. Go through another kissing gate and continue along the field-edge to a kissing gate on the right, halfway up the field. Cross a footbridge and stile, turn left, and head diagonally right uphill, making for a gap in the trees. Go up the slope to a broad drive, veer right and pass a waymarker as you emerge from the woodland onto a drive (where cars may be parked).

5 Branch half left at the next waymarker, and take the grassy path across the slopes. Head for a kissing gate to the right of three tall Wellingtonias and follow the path across pasture, towards woodland. Head for a kissing gate, pick your way through the trees to a drive and cross over towards Waddesdon. Pass garages and an ornate house with the five arrows emblem before emerging at the road. Turn right onto the High Street and continue for a few paces to return to Baker Street.

WHERE TO EAT AND DRINK Within Waddesdon Manor grounds is the Manor Restaurant, with table service, and the informal self-service Stables Café. On the High Street, The Long Dog has the most interesting menu, including tapas, and borders on gastro-pub classification.

WHAT TO SEE The modern Rothschild Foundation building on Windmill Hill is the focal point for Lord Rothschild's philanthropic concerns. These range from interests in international affairs such as the Middle East to local initiatives, providing grants to charities across a range of sectors in the Vale of Aylesbury. The building has been awarded a prestigious regional RIBA award. It is open on Friday afternoons during the summer.

WHILE YOU'RE THERE Waddesdon Manor can easily keep you occupied for half a day, and possibly a lot longer. Aside from its many acres of beautiful gardens, it boasts a world-class collection of art, porcelain, carpets and tapestries, all housed inside a stunning Renaissance-style château, with interiors inspired by 18th-century France. The house is open from Tuesday to Sunday.

Ivinghoe Beacon and the Ridgeway

DISTANCE 4 miles (6.4km)	MINIMUM TIME 1hr 45min

ASCENT/GRADIENT 280ft (85m) ▲▲▲   LEVEL OF DIFFICULTY ✚✚✦

PATHS Farmland and woodland paths, some road walking; several stiles

LANDSCAPE Mix of remote farmland and typical Chiltern scenery

SUGGESTED MAP AA Walker's Map 24 The Chilterns

START/FINISH Grid reference: SP962162

DOG FRIENDLINESS Lead required across farmland

PARKING Official car park near Ivinghoe Beacon

PUBLIC TOILETS None on route

Ivinghoe Beacon is a suitably dramatic setting for the start of the Ridgeway, the ancient trade route that was once busy with travellers. Cattle drovers used it regularly, as did locals on short journeys, long-distance traders and pilgrims.

THE RIDGEWAY TRAIL

The Ridgeway trail extends for 85 miles (137km) through the Buckinghamshire Chilterns to the Thames, and then across Berkshire and into Wiltshire. In places the trail is as wide as a main road or a dual carriageway. When the original line became weathered or difficult to negotiate, travellers moved from one side to the other, gradually making the track wider. The character of the Ridgeway changes the further west you travel. Initially, the trail cuts through beechwood scenery – glorious in autumn – and across soft rolling hills. Over the Thames, the landscape assumes a totally different character. From the river onwards, the Ridgeway cuts across bleak, exposed downland, offering little in the way of shelter on a wet or windy day. This stretch of the Ridgeway passes through a landscape littered with long barrows, prehistoric forts and monuments.

A RIDGED LANDSCAPE

The downs of Berkshire and Wiltshire and the softer country of the Chilterns are remnants of a landscape of huge domes and ridges formed around 25 million years ago. The upper strata consists of great ridges of chalk laid down in the sea probably more than 60 million years ago.

Whether you are interested in history or geology, a walk along the Ridgeway is a journey through time. You can walk for miles without seeing another soul, following in the footsteps of 300 generations and enjoying the views of the same tracts of chalk downland, the same distant hills and the same broad river. Today, walkers can follow the route from start to finish, but that hasn't always been the case. In 1942 the Ramblers Association proposed a long distance route across this part of southern England, but it was another 30 years before it was officially opened to the public. With its access to villages and overnight accommodation, many people choose the Ridgeway for a very pleasant walking holiday, allowing up to a week to complete the route at a leisurely pace.

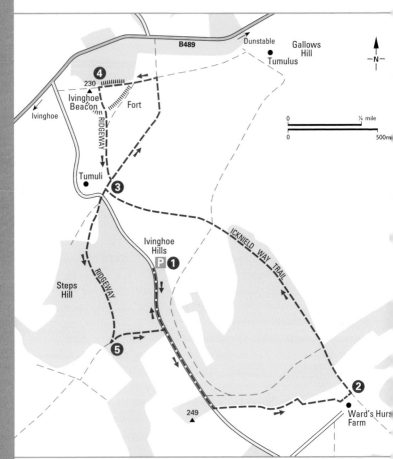

❶ Leave the car park for the road and keep left. Pass a track on the left and cross a cattle grid. Continue ahead to a field gate and waymarker sign on the left. Go straight ahead, with the fence on the left. At the bottom of the field keep to the right of a mound of debris and enter the next field. Veer half left, heading to

the left of Ward's Hurst Farm. Go through a kissing gate. At the next kissing gate turn left, then go through a gate and keep the fence on your right. (The right of way has recently been modified here; if you find yourself heading down the hill at this point you have gone wrong.)

2 Continue ahead, passing under power lines, to a kissing gate, and turn left onto the Icknield Way through the Ashridge Estate. Follow the waymarked trail, including a steep descent of steps, through woodland to a kissing gate and continue ahead, still on the Icknield Way, avoiding the Boundary Trail branching off to the right. Through a kissing gate keep the fence on your left, climbing gently via two kissing gates to a marker stone for the Icknield Way, the Peddars Way and the Ridgeway.

3 Turn sharp right to a kissing gate and gate, and follow a clear track striking out across expansive downland. By a fence corner, head up the steep slope to the ridge and bear left along it to a kissing gate. This stretch of the walk offers grand views of Ivinghoe Beacon and the surrounding countryside. Walk ahead along the ridge at the Ridgeway sign, making for the start of the National Trail.

4 With your back to the Ridgeway plinth, follow the trail as it runs south. Descend steeply, keep left at the fork and make for the road. Cross over and continue on the National Trail, beginning a moderate climb. Go through a kissing gate and cut between trees before spotting a deep combe cutting into the hillside on the right. Pass two stiles by gates, and when the Ridgeway sweeps right by a waymarker, bear left.

5 Cross a track just beyond it and follow the woodland footpath until you reach the drive to Clipper Down Cottage. Join the road here, turn left and return to the car park.

WHERE TO EAT AND DRINK There are no pubs on the route of the walk, but a short drive away in the attractive village of Ivinghoe is the Rose and Crown. This lovely 17th-century inn, complete with barn and coach yard (now the garden bar), serves local ales and good food.

WHAT TO SEE While following the Ridgeway, look to the west for a view of Pitstone Windmill. Believed to date back to 1627, it is probably the oldest surviving windmill in the country. It was in a derelict state when the National Trust took it over in 1937. It has since been restored by volunteers and is now open to the public.

WHILE YOU'RE THERE The walk crosses the magnificent National Trust Ashridge Estate, which includes a variety of woodlands, commons and chalk downland, with all manner of wildlife and superb scenery.

From Brill to Little London

DISTANCE 4 miles (6.4km)	MINIMUM TIME 1hr 30min
ASCENT/GRADIENT 350ft (107m) ▲▲▲	LEVEL OF DIFFICULTY +++
PATHS Field paths and tracks, several stretches of road; several stiles	
LANDSCAPE Mixture of farmland and rolling country	
SUGGESTED MAP OS Explorer 180 Oxford	
START/FINISH Grid reference: SP653141	
DOG FRIENDLINESS Lead required around livestock	
PARKING Room to park by windmill	
PUBLIC TOILETS None on route	

After successfully holding up the night mail train from Glasgow to London in the early hours of Thursday 8 August, 1963 (see Walk 7), the Great Train Robbers journeyed 27 or so miles (43.5km) west across country to a farm near the village of Brill. This was to be their hideout, where they could lay low for a day or two after the robbery.

REMOTE HIDEAWAY

Leatherslade Farm was just what they wanted – remotely situated on high ground and well away from the road. The men chose the site in the same way that the Romans and the people of the Iron Age chose their hilltop settlements – so they could spot any sign of an approaching enemy. Initially they had considered using a fleet of high-powered, 3.8-litre engined Jaguars as getaway cars. That way they could be back in London in an hour. But driving at high speed through Buckinghamshire's country lanes in the middle of the night was perhaps not the wisest option. After careful consideration, they hit upon the idea of looking for a suitable hideout within half an hour's drive of the hold-up site.

In June the men spotted a farm advertised in the local press and after viewing it, made an offer of £5,550, which was accepted. The owners moved out at the end of July and a week later, on the morning of Tuesday 6 August, members of the gang began to arrive at the farm. By midnight the following evening they were ready for action.

A CLEAN SWEEP

They returned to Leatherslade Farm after the train robbery and began digging a hole in the garden to bury the mailbags. They cleaned the farm from top to bottom, wiping down the surfaces and burning all the shoes and clothes that had been worn during the raid. Using several vans to carry the money, the gang eventually left the farm late on the Friday night – nearly 48 hours after the robbery.

The following Monday, a local farm labourer noticed the blacked-out windows. Climbing through the hedge into the yard, he spotted a five-ton army truck in the shed. He rang the police, who were busy taking up to 400 train robbery-related calls a day. Eventually they arrived, and discovered numerous clues indicating that this had been the Great Train Robbers' hideout. But they needed proof, and the gang had removed any incriminating evidence that could link them to the farm – or so they thought. Ronald Biggs had left his prints on a ketchup bottle in the kitchen. It was just what the police had been looking for.

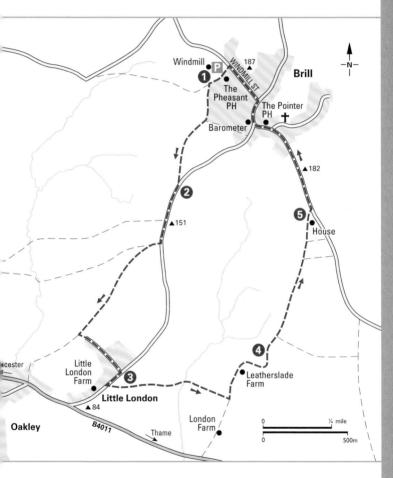

❶ Go down South Hills Lane, beside The Pheasant, with the windmill on your right. At a private garage and a waymarker post, swing left to join a track. Follow it as it curves round to the right to a pair of garages, and enter an enclosed footpath, right. This is very narrow, and may be overgrown and boggy; there are wooden stepping blocks. Keep to the enclosed footpath and head over three stiles before crossing rolling grassland. Head straight across the field (no path) towards a large house and a kissing-gate to the left. Go through the gate and turn right onto the road.

2 Pass a public footpath sign on the right, then just before a bend, on the right, is a small parking area leading to a bridleway. It is waymarked but this may be obscured by trees. Go 50yds (45m) along the track, then look left for a stile and cross into the field. Head diagonally right over the brow (no path) and down the field to a plank bridge and stile. Aim left down the adjoining field, making for a metal kissing gate just to the right of a large cream-coloured house with dormer windows. Turn left and follow a footpath towards the cottage. Keep left, cross the grassy frontage of the end house, walk along the lane to the main road and turn right.

3 Take the first path left, opposite Little London Farm. Over a stile, head diagonally left into the field (no path), pass under power lines and make for the right-hand of two steel field gates. Go through and cross the field, walking straight ahead to a waymarker and a galvanised field gate. Continue ahead across the next pasture to a metal kissing-gate and track. (The farm below, right, is London Farm.) Turn left uphill towards Leatherslade Farm and take the narrow, overgrown bridlepath to the left of the farm gates, signed 'Beware Guard Dogs'. Go between hedges, and skirt the house and outbuildings. The present Leatherslade Farm House was built to replace the original farmhouse used by the gang during the robbery.

4 Once clear of the farmhouse buildings, the overgrown bridleway bears left and keeps climbing, passing a boarded gate right, then a junction with wooden farm gates to left and right. Continue and eventually come to a galvanised gate. Continue ahead, with the field boundary on your right. Pass several more footpaths on the right and keep going until you reach a field gate in the top boundary. Follow the track ahead to the road by the entrance to a house.

5 Keep left here and walk along the road to Brill. Pass the chapel; over to the right across the green is the village church and The Pointer pub. Pass a turning on the left to Oakley and look for the barometer in the wall. Bear left into Windmill Street and return to the car park.

WHERE TO EAT AND DRINK There are a couple of very attractive and characterful pubs in Brill. At the start of the walk, The Pheasant serves superior pub food and has a panoramic terrace that overlooks the windmill. At the end of the walk, The Pointer serves sandwiches at lunchtime alongside gastropub meals, and has its own butcher's (Thursday to Saturday) selling the highest quality meat and charcuterie.

WHAT TO SEE Almost at the end of the walk, just beyond the turning to Oakley, is a rare surviving example of a public barometer. Set in the wall, it dates back to 1910 (and may not be accurate!). It was erected in memory of Sir Edmund Verney of Claydon House (see Walk 6) in recognition of his service to Brill and district as a county councillor.

WHILE YOU'RE THERE Brill Windmill is perhaps the oldest mill of its kind in the country. It dates from around 1680 and is a post mill – a type of windmill whose whole body revolves around a central post to face the wind. It was last used in 1919 for milling barley. It is open to visitors on Sundays from Easter (or April) until September.

From the Hartwells to the River Thame

DISTANCE 5 miles (8km)	MINIMUM TIME 2hrs

ASCENT/GRADIENT 180ft (55m) ▲▲▲   LEVEL OF DIFFICULTY ✚✚✚

PATHS Field and riverside paths, tracks and lanes; several stiles

LANDSCAPE Gently rolling farmland and villages south of River Thame

SUGGESTED MAP AA Walker's Map 24 The Chilterns

START/FINISH Grid reference: SP783123

DOG FRIENDLINESS Lead required near Lower Hartwell Farm and alongside River Thame

PARKING Space in Eythrope Road, Upper Hartwell

PUBLIC TOILETS None on route

'Why wouldst thou leave calm Hartwell's green abode...
Apician table and Horatian Ode?'

So wrote Lord Byron on Louis XVIII's departure for France to assume his throne in 1814.

Few hotels can boast such a royal connection, but it was in the library of Hartwell House, just outside Aylesbury, that its most famous resident, Louis XVIII, exiled King of France, signed the accession papers to the throne. Louis leased the house between 1809 and 1814, staying here with his court during the Napoleonic Wars. The Queen of France died here during this period, and her coffin was taken from Hartwell to Sardinia.

HARTWELL HOUSE

One of England's finest stately homes and grandest country hotels, Hartwell House was built for the Hampden and Lee families, ancestors of the American Civil War soldier, General Robert E Lee, during the 17th and 18th centuries. Now a Grade I-listed building, the house has many Jacobean and Georgian features, magnificent decorative plasterwork, ceilings and panelling, fine paintings and antique furniture.

The philanthropist Ernest Edward Cook (grandson of tourism pioneer Thomas Cook), an important benefactor of the National Trust and National Art Collections Fund, bought Hartwell House and its estate from the Lees in 1938. He was also a founder of the Ernest Cook Trust, which, in the mid-1980s, made Hartwell House and its parkland available to Historic House Hotels for a major restoration and conversion. Only hotel guests can proceed beyond the main gates, so if you want to see inside Hartwell, book in for dinner or afternoon tea.

The entrance to the house is via a porch flanked by pillars of carved stone and a carved doorway. Set above all this is a splendid oriel window sitting on intricately embroidered stone corbels. The Great Hall is an imposing room in English baroque style, built by James Gibbs in 1740. The rococo Morning Room with its decorated ceiling and door cases, the adjoining Drawing Room and the Library, are all Georgian and date from about 1760. The principal Dining Room was added in the 1980s by Eric Throssell when a major conversion took place, and reflects the style of the early 19th-century architect Sir John Soane. Hartwell's proximity to Chequers (Walk 13) means that it has frequently hosted international summits and important government meetings.

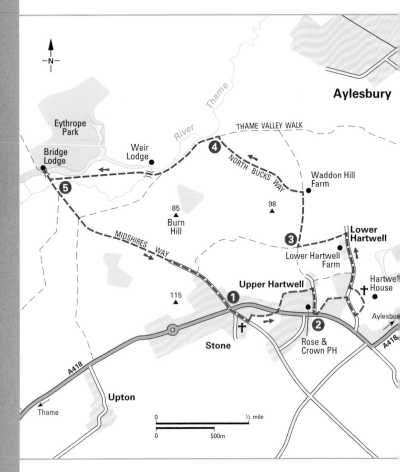

❶ From the A418, turn into Bishopstone Road and keep to the left of the church. Go through a kissing gate and walk along to the footpath beside Manor Farm Close. Cross to a gate leading out to a recreation ground. The gate pillars, left, recall the villagers who died in the two World Wars. Exit to the road, cross over to a footpath sign and follow the drive. Just before a garage and shed, turn right and follow the path round.

Go through a gate and follow the path to the road. Turn right, walk to the A418, with the Rose and Crown to the right.

② Turn sharp left at the corner and follow the path beside a wall. Head for the road, bear right and walk along to Hartwell House. Note the ornate bridge to the right, but go left (with the Spa Café and Bar to the right), and at the gate take the path beside the pillar on the left. Go through a kissing gate, pass the church, right, and the graveyard, left. Turn right at the road and pass the Egyptian Well. Continue ahead to pass Lower Hartwell Farm, then turn left at the footpath. Cross a stile and two fields, walking straight ahead, then turn right immediately after crossing a plank bridge.

③ Skirt the field, keeping the hedge on your left, and continue ahead on the North Bucks Way, heading towards Waddon Hill Farm. At the farm buildings turn left at the waymarker and follow the track out across the fields. Keep alongside a hedge initially, then go through one field and enter another. When the path veers left, branch off right along a narrow path through an arable field, making for a gate. Go through the squeeze stile alongside it and cross a meadow to reach the River Thame. Swing left at the river bank to a gate and join the Thame Valley Walk.

④ After about 100yds (91m) go through a second gate. The path follows a stream (perhaps hidden, right) to the next gate, where you rejoin the river bank. Follow the Thame, continuing on the waymarked trail. Pass a broken kissing gate and go over a footbridge, then cross another footbridge at a weir. Opposite is lovely Weir Lodge. Join a concrete track via a stile and follow it towards some trees.

⑤ Once in the trees, the Thame is on the left. To the right is the parkland of Eythrope. At the next junction take a short detour right and cross a picturesque bridge to see Bridge Lodge. Retrace your steps, go straight through the gates, and follow a long walk along the tarmac drive, with a moderate lengthy ascent, eventually passing through gates at the crest, before reaching your car.

WHERE TO EAT AND DRINK The Spa Café and Bar at Hartwell House serves coffee as well as lunch and is a nice place to sample the hotel's grandeur informally. Or you could opt for the grander afternoon tea. The Rose and Crown at Hartwell is another option – the pub underwent major refurbishments in 2013.

WHAT TO SEE The Hartwell Estate boasts many treasures and curiosities. The bridge over the lake, erected at the end of the 19th century, is the central span of old Kew Bridge, built in the 18th century by James Paine. Outside the main door of the house stands an equestrian statue of Frederick, Prince of Wales, and on the walk you'll see an Egyptian-style pavilion of 1851 over a spring.

WHILE YOU'RE THERE St Mary's Church, in the grounds of Hartwell House, was built between 1754 and 1756 by Henry Keene and is a splendid example of Gothic revival, modeled on the Chapter House of York Minster. Enquire at the hotel reception regarding access.

A ramble at Chequers

DISTANCE 5 miles (8km)   MINIMUM TIME 2hrs

ASCENT/GRADIENT 378ft (115m) ▲▲▲   LEVEL OF DIFFICULTY ✚✚✚

PATHS Field and woodland paths and tracks, stretch of Ridgeway; many stiles

LANDSCAPE Chiltern country, a mixture of rolling hills and woodland

SUGGESTED MAP AA Walker's Map 24 The Chilterns

START/FINISH Grid reference: SP842069

DOG FRIENDLINESS Lead required through villages and on short road stretches

PARKING Limited spaces at Butler's Cross

PUBLIC TOILETS None on route

In an age when politicians and world leaders live with the constant threat of terrorist attacks, it is perhaps a little surprising that you can take a country walk through the grounds of Chequers – the Prime Minister's official country seat near Princes Risborough. The Ridgeway cuts across its picturesque parkland, almost like a symbol of our democratic heritage, passing within sight of Chequers and offering superb views of the house and its glorious Chiltern setting.

WEEKEND RETREAT OR FORTRESS?

But don't be fooled. When the PM chooses Chequers to host a summit or entertain a world leader, you can be sure that the security forces will have it sealed like a drum. Surveillance is usually discreet and understated – there might not be armed guards and security barriers as far as the eye can see, but you are being watched.

Take a walk in the surrounding countryside and chances are you'll strike up a conversation with people who claim to have seen police combing the woods in search of terrorists or cranks. Others say they have seen two identical convoys of ministerial cars and Special Branch 4x4 vehicles leaving Chequers – one presumably carrying the PM and his staff, the other a possible decoy. Fact or fiction, it all adds to the romance and mystery of Chequers and provides plenty of fodder for writers of political thrillers.

GIFTED TO THE NATION

Built in 1565, the house was given to the nation in 1921 by Viscount Lee of Fareham. He wrote:

'...the better the health of our rulers the more sanely they will rule, and the inducement to spend two days a week in the high and pure air of the Chiltern hills and woods will, it is hoped, benefit the nation as well as its chosen leaders.'

Lady Mary Grey, sister of the ill-fated Lady Jane, was initially confined here in disgrace by Elizabeth I after marrying Thomas Keys without her consent. Civil War battles were fought in this part of the country and the house contains one of the finest collections of relics from that period, though sadly they are not seen by the public.

Not all prime ministers have been impressed by Chequers. Bonar Law disliked the country, but Clement Attlee loved it and even bought a house in the area. Ramsay McDonald described it as 'this house of comforting and regenerating rest', but it was Winston Churchill who summed it up best: 'what momentous meetings it has witnessed, what fateful decisions have been taken under this roof'.

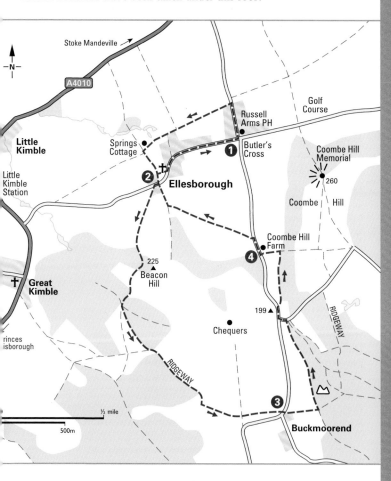

❶ From Butler's Cross follow Chalkshire Road, keeping the Russell Arms pub on the right. At a row of cottages take the path opposite, signposted 'Aylesbury Ring'. Cross two stiles, continue ahead to a drive on a bend and keep ahead, passing Springs Cottage. Continue ahead into a field through a kissing gate, keep to the left and after a few paces is a stile on the left. Climb over and make the steep ascent up the slope to Ellesborough

Church. Go through a kissing gate and up a long flight of steps and keep to the right of the church. Cross a stile, then cross the road to a bus stop, go right for several paces, then left through a kissing gate.

② Follow the path straight up the slope to a kissing gate, heading to the right of Beacon Hill. Go through a gate and continue through some trees. Take the grassy path which veers right and passes to the right of the summit of the hill; once over the brow it becomes a chalk path. Go into the trees, then ascend a long steep flight of steps. Cross a meadow, go back into more trees and cross a track that leads to Chequers. Go through a kissing gate into a field and keep to the left edge. Leave the field by another gate and join the Ridgeway path. Chequers is now in full view to your left. Follow the path, and shortly after you enter trees turn left at the Ridgeway waymarker. Cross the field and a drive, via three gates, and continue across another field to a road.

③ Cross the road and follow the Ridgeway through woodland. On reaching a four-way junction, turn left and follow the path along the side of the hill. After a while a number of paths converge by the road. Turn left at the road, then right where it joins Missenden Road. Keep to the right pavement and pass a lodge house. As the road bends off left, follow the path straight ahead/right. Continue through woodland, and just before a gate onto Coombe Hill bear left, down a short slope, and follow the path, then a drive, to the road by Coombe Hill Farm.

④ Turn right, cross to a pavement, and after 150yds (135m) turn left to a wooden barrier to join a long path through a large field. After a hundred paces or so, look back over your right shoulder and up towards the hill, to Coombe Hill Memorial. Bear right at a track, following it to the road opposite Ellesborough Church. Enter the churchyard, keep to the right of the church and make for a gate. Pass some cottages on the left, go downhill to the pavement and walk along the road to return to Butler's Cross.

WHERE TO EAT AND DRINK The Russell Arms at Butler's Cross has modernised the traditional country inn with some quirky decor and staff who have a real desire to please. They offer highly rated gastropub cuisine and have brought old snack favourites, such as pork pies and Scotch eggs, into the 21st century. They also stock an excellent range of local real ales.

WHAT TO SEE Keep your eye on the skyline and you'll notice Coombe Hill Memorial several times along the route, most memorably towards the end of the walk. The highest accessible viewpoint in the Chilterns, the grand 60ft (18.3m) monument is a memorial to Buckinghamshire men who died in South Africa during the Boer War (see Walk 14).

WHILE YOU'RE THERE Have a look at Ellesborough Church. It may be locked but outside, above the porch, are figures indicating it is dedicated to St Peter and St Paul. There's been a church here for centuries, but the present building was heavily restored in Victorian times. Past prime ministers have worshipped here and even read the lesson. On Sunday and bank holiday afternoons you can not only visit the tower, but also enjoy tea and cake here.

Up Coombe Hill

DISTANCE 4 miles (6.4km)   MINIMUM TIME 2hrs 30min

ASCENT/GRADIENT 354ft (108m) ▲▲▲   LEVEL OF DIFFICULTY ✚✚✚

PATHS Wendover town centre, field and woodland paths and tracks; several stiles

LANDSCAPE Chiltern country, a mixture of rolling hills and woodland

SUGGESTED MAP AA Walker's Map 24 The Chilterns

START/FINISH Grid reference: SP869078

DOG FRIENDLINESS Lead required in town

PARKING High Street car park

PUBLIC TOILETS High Street car park

The old market town of Wendover is a popular and pretty commuter settlement, with a frequent train service to London Marylebone. The regular route to London, some 40 miles (64km) southeast, is nothing new. In the early 1800s a stagecoach ran to Holborn from the Red Lion on the High Street. Long before that the ancient Icknield Way trade route, one of the oldest roads in the country, passed right through the town and brought prosperity. In 1533 Henry VIII's recorder, John Leland, visited Wendover and recorded, 'A town having two streets, well builded with tymbre'. It remains essentially a two-street town, built around the axis of High Street/Tring Road and Aylesbury Road, and many timber properties remain, albeit remodelled over the centuries. Behind the landmark Clock Tower at the bottom of the High Street flows the chalk stream that gives Wendover its name (it means 'white waters'); a watermill, first recorded in the Domesday Book, last worked in 1923, is also to be found here.

Today, a much noisier route than the old stagecoach threatens to disrupt Wendover's peace and quiet, if the High Speed 2 (HS2) rail line from London to the Midlands takes its proposed route immediately west of the town, passing through a tunnel and across viaducts uncomfortably close to the town centre.

COOMBE HILL

Just a short walk from the centre, Coombe Hill – 106 acres (43ha) of downland – rises 852ft (260m) above sea level and is the highest accessible viewpoint in the Chilterns. The 60ft (18.3m) monument atop the hill is a memorial to 148 men of Buckinghamshire who died in South Africa during the Boer War (1899–1902). Erected by public subscription in 1904, it was struck by lightning in 1938 and later rebuilt. In 1972 the bronze tablet attached to the memorial was stolen. A stone one replaces it.

There are magnificent views from here over a sizeable area of the county, particularly the Aylesbury Vale, with Aylesbury some 5 miles (8km) due north. Gliders often swoop silently into view in the skies above. Almost immediately west is Pulpit Hill, home to the remains of an ancient hill-fort. Chequers, the country home of the Prime Minister, lies 0.75 miles (1.2km) in this direction (see Walk 13). From the Coombe Hill Memorial it is hidden by trees, but if you walk approximately 100yds (90m) left of the monument, along the Ridgeway trail, and look down to the left, you can see the house.

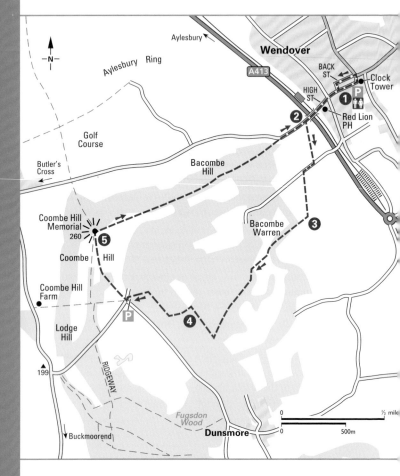

❶ Turn right out of the High Street car park to visit the tourist office, housed in the distinctive Clock Tower, which was built as a small market hall in 1842. Pick up a town trail map here. Cross (with care) the Aylesbury Road diagonally to walk up Back Street, parallel to the High Street. Once part of the ancient Icknield Way, Back Street is still lined with old traders' cottages dating from the 16th, 17th and 18th centuries. At Dobbins Lane turn left, then right back onto the High Street, and pass the railway station. Cross the road, and once you are over the bridge, look for a waymarked footpath left.

❷ Go over two stiles, towards pylons. Head diagonally right across the field to go over another stile. Turn right uphill along the lane. After about 90yds (82m) turn left, following the bridleway beside a modern house, and go along the track as it swings round to the right, passing a stile (marked private). Go to the end of the field and turn right through a metal gate.

❸ Follow the path between wire fences as it first dips then sweeps uphill, for around 0.75 miles (1.2km). As the track flattens out, turn right onto a bridleway. After about 160yds (146m) cross a private drive. The path ahead splits – take the right-hand footpath with the fence to your right. After around 200yds (183m) turn sharp left at a waymarker post along a muddy footpath, following the yellow arrows painted on the trees through the wood. In late spring there is a spectacular carpet of bluebells here.

❹ Follow this path until the next waymarker at a T-junction. Turn right and continue ahead for around 275yds (251m), then turn left at the next waymarker and follow the path through a short, dark, wooded area to Coombe Hill and a National Trust car park. Go through the gate, pass a picnic area (right), and take the footpath which veers to the left and goes across the plateau to reach the monument.

❺ After enjoying the spectacular views across the Vale of Aylesbury, continue right, following the black Ridgeway waymarker post (just below you). The route now descends slowly via a series of gates and, close to the road, a flight of steps, all the way back down to the road. At the road, turn right and continue past the railway station to the High Street. Note the lovely old Tudor houses on the right, once the old post office, now housing antiques dealers, and further along, on the left, Rumsey's Chocolaterie, set in an old bank. Return to the car park.

WHERE TO EAT AND DRINK There are many choices of refreshments in Wendover, from a three-course meal in 17th-century cottages to drinking chocolate on the upper floor of an old bank, to having a pint of beer in the same inn (the Red Lion) where Oliver Cromwell, Robert Louis Stevenson and Rupert Brooke have all stayed. In summer shop in Wendover for picnic supplies to eat on Coombe Hill.

WHAT TO SEE The National Trust, who manage Coombe Hill, use the eye-catching heritage breed of black-and-white belted Galloway cattle to keep the scrub down and the grass low so that other species can thrive.

WHILE YOU'RE THERE Wendover Woods, east of the town, is the highest point in the Chilterns – at 870ft (265m), slightly higher than Coombe Hill, though not as spectacular. Ornithologists come here to spot the rare firecrest, which vies with the goldcrest for the title of the UK's smallest bird. Families can enjoy the Go Ape tree-top aerial walkway.

Overleaf: View from the Chiltern escarpment at Coombe Hill (Walk 14)

Following Roald Dahl at Great Missenden

DISTANCE 4.25 miles (6.8km)   MINIMUM TIME 2hrs

ASCENT/GRADIENT 85ft (26m) ▲▲▲   LEVEL OF DIFFICULTY ✚✚✚

PATHS Field paths, stretches of road, one flight of steps

LANDSCAPE Farmland, woods, pasture, and landscaped grounds and lake of Missenden Abbey

SUGGESTED MAP OS Explorer 181 Chiltern Hills North

START/FINISH Grid reference: SP895015

DOG FRIENDLINESS Under control across farmland and in wildlife conservation area

PARKING Link Road car park

PUBLIC TOILETS Link Road car park

The pretty little village of Great Missenden has two claims to fame. Missenden Abbey, founded in 1133, served as a monastery for over 400 years until ruined in the Reformation. The ruins were later incorporated into a Georgian mansion, but this was gutted by fire in 1985. Now restored, it functions as a centre for conferences and adult education, and as a wedding and events venue. You can wander into its front entrance, enjoy the views and enquire at reception if the building is free to look around.

AN AUTHOR'S INSPIRATION

Its second claim to fame is as the home of one of the world's best-selling children's authors. Roald Dahl was born in Wales in 1916, to Norwegian parents, and served with distinction in the RAF during World War II. He wrote about his wartime adventures and his first book was published in 1942. His first children's book, *The Gremlins*, was published a year later. In 1954 he moved to Great Missenden and lived at Gipsy Cottage until his death in 1990. He used Angling Spring Wood as inspiration for *Fantastic Mr Fox*, and Atkins Wood in *Danny the Champion of the World*. With such classics as *James and the Giant Peach, Charlie and the Chocolate Factory, Matilda, The Witches, The Twits* and *The BFG* to his name, he is regarded as one of the all-time great children's storytellers. Dahl contributed to the screenplays for two Ian Fleming novels, *Chitty Chitty Bang Bang* (creating the creepy 'Childcatcher' character) and *You Only Live Twice*. He also gained fame for his dark, often macabre, adult short stories, which often included a twist in the tale.

Great Missenden's High Street will be familiar to readers of *Danny the Champion of the World*, for the 'Red Pump Garage', featuring two splendid old petrol pumps ('Sorry, out of fuel ever since 8 gallons went over £1...'). And No. 70, Crown House, was the inspiration for Sophie's 'norphanage' in *The BFG*. You can pay your respects to the author at the Church of St Peter and St Paul, where he is buried just below the memorial bench in the shade of the trees. In typical Dahl humour, note the concrete footprints of the BFG next to the author's simple gravestone.

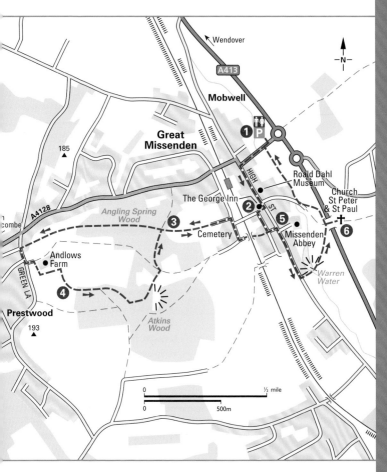

❶ Exit the car park right, then turn left onto the High Street. Continue past the 'Red Pump Garage' and the Roald Dahl Museum and Story Centre to reach The George Inn. Take the alleyway on the right (signed 'BASDA and ART recruitment') immediately before it. At the end, turn left onto an unmade road, with the 400-year-old timbers of the rear of The George Inn to your left.

❷ Soon turn left onto Twitchell Road. Turn right onto Whitefield Lane, which leads beneath the railway. Turn immediately right onto unmade

Trafford Road (you may spot Gipsy House on your right), then turn left after 50yds (46m) onto a waymarked track. Pass a cemetery on the left. The gate ahead leads to open fields and woods. Go straight ahead, keeping the fence on your left, to a gate entering Angling Spring Wood.

❸ Continue straight on through the wood. Leave it via a kissing gate and take the path straight ahead, bisecting a field, and emerging onto the road at Green Lane. Turn left, walk a few paces to Andlows Farm and turn left into here. After a few steps (before the farm buildings) turn sharp right at the corner of the hedge, and go through a gate with the farmhouse on the left. At the next gate turn left, still keeping the farmhouse to your left. You soon enter Atkins Wood.

❹ The path forks and the broader trail leads right; take the less obvious path left, which keeps close to the left-hand perimeter of the beech wood. At the end of the wood go through a kissing gate and turn left onto a bridleway. This leads to a tarmac lane and on past the entrance to Angling Spring Farm. The lane bends right, but take the track left with a panoramic view from here towards Great Missenden.

Continue ahead into Angling Spring Wood, following a steep path downhill. Veer right and rejoin the trail on which you entered the woods. Retrace your steps back via the railway tunnel and continue to the end of Whitefield Lane.

❺ Turn right onto High Street and cross the road. After around 70yds (64m) is the entrance to Missenden Abbey. Continue straight on, and turn left at the waymarker through a kissing gate. Almost immediately on your left is a small humpback bridge which offers a great view of the abbey across Warren Water. Leave by another gate and continue on the path, leading uphill, to the right of the abbey. Go through a gate at the top of the field, ascend some steps and go straight ahead, crossing the bridge over the A413 to visit the church and graveyard.

❻ Retrace your steps back to the bridge and go straight on, following Church Lane. Walk past two cottages, and turn right, then immediately left. Follow the road round to the left, with Oldham Hall and the school on your right. As the road ends, follow the footpath. This leads into the playing fields directly opposite Link Road car park – cross them to return to the start.

WHERE TO EAT AND DRINK There are numerous choices, from two dining pubs to more basic pub food at The George, a cafe at either end of the High Street, and the Café Twit for children, at the Roald Dahl Museum. On summer Sundays cream teas are served at the church and at Missenden Abbey.

WHAT TO SEE Roald Dahl's widow, Felicity, still lives in Gipsy House, which you may be able to glimpse from near the railway. The house is strictly private (please do not disturb), but opens to the public on a few days each year under the National Gardens Scheme. See their website for details.

WHILE YOU'RE THERE The Roald Dahl Museum and Story Centre (closed Mondays) was established by Roald Dahl's widow, Felicity, in 1991. It delights tens of thousands of children (and parents) who visit each year and who no doubt agree with the words above the museum (from *The BFG*): 'it is truly swizzfigglingly flushbunkingly gloriumptious'. Note the Willy Wonka gates just inside the archway.

Chesham and the Chess Valley

DISTANCE 5 miles (8km)   MINIMUM TIME 2hrs 15min

ASCENT/GRADIENT 165ft (50m) ▲▲▲   LEVEL OF DIFFICULTY ✚✚✚

PATHS Roads, field and woodland paths and tracks

LANDSCAPE Unspoiled farmland and woodland scenery

SUGGESTED MAP AA Walker's Map 24 The Chilterns

START/FINISH Grid reference: SP960016

DOG FRIENDLINESS Lead required in villages and around livestock, and on train

PARKING Chesham Underground Station

PUBLIC TOILETS Chesham Underground Station; Chalfont and Latimer Underground Station

NOTES This route returns to the start point at Chesham via train on the Metropolitan Line from Chalfont and Latimer Station

If you're not familiar with Buckinghamshire, it's something of a surprise to arrive at a small country town and find signs for London Underground. Chesham lies at the very end of a branch of the Metropolitan Line, which opened in 1889. Together with nearby Amersham, it's one of London Underground's furthest outposts.

Work began on extending what was then known as the St John's Wood Line beyond central London during the latter years of the 19th century. By the mid-1880s the railway had become known as the Metropolitan, running 17.5 miles (28km) from Baker Street. The plan was to continue the line all the way to Aylesbury, but financial problems restricted its extension to Chesham.

CIVIC SUPPORT

Most of the land for the new sections of railway was acquired from the Duke of Bedford and Lord Chesham, but the land for the final 0.5 miles (800m) of the Chesham branch was presented to the railway by local residents of the town, who were keen that a station should built in the town centre rather than on the outskirts, as was originally planned. In May 1889 the people of Chesham were invited to inspect the branch and afterwards entertained to a banquet. Seven weeks later, the line from Rickmansworth to Chesham was opened. For the next three years, until the main line from Chalfont and Latimer Station to Amersham and Aylesbury was opened in 1892, Chesham was the Metropolitan's most northerly terminus.

Today, commuters still board the train and travel 25 miles (40km) to Aldgate in the City of London via places like Finchley

Road, Northwood Hills, Wembley Park and Pinner – the very heart of Metroland In 'Summoned by Bells' (1960) John Betjeman wrote, 'Metroland/Beckoned us out to lanes in beechy Bucks', and before that, in 'The Metropolitan Railway', he enthused:

> *'Early Electric! With what radiant hope*
> *Men formed this many-branched electrolier.'*

RIVER POWER

Chesham lies on the sparkling River Chess, a chalk stream with its clear water coming from the groundwater held in the Chiltern Hills. From the 10th century onwards water mills on the Chess Valley were the driving force of the local economy.

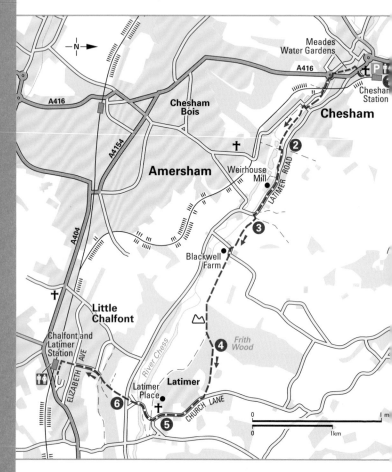

❶ Take the alleyway to the right of the station. Bear right at the waymarker, down to the Baptist Church. Cross the road, bear slightly left and follow the path to the left

through Meades Water Gardens to a roundabout. Take the first exit, Moor Road, and pass beneath the railway. Continue straight on along the path by the river. Swing right at the next footbridge and rejoin the road. Pass 'Gym and Swim', go straight ahead, then cross a small concrete bridge into a playing field.

❷ Skirt the left boundary of the field, then follow the gap in the hedge, left, and rejoin the river. Cross a wooden footbridge and continue on the path, criss-crossing between branches of the river. Cross the river again by a weir. The path is running parallel to Latimer Road and soon joins it. Continue along the road, passing Weirhouse Mill. Go past Milk Hall Barns and ignore the footpath left, but as the road swings right, veer off left through a kissing-gate, signed 'Blackwell Hall'.

❸ Keep to the right-hand (bottom) edge of the field, and continue straight ahead through fields to a paddock with horses. Exit by a wooden gate. Go straight ahead past Blackwell Farm, turn left and, as the lane sweeps left, continue straight ahead on a track. Go through a blue metal gate and past farm outbuildings, with views right. Continue over farmland through three fields, to reach a gate into woods. Follow the path leading right, uphill, with a barbed wire fence immediately to your right. The narrow, steep path eventually swings slightly left, where it broadens out. At the woodland edge emerge at a large field.

❹ Skirt the field, keeping the trees on your right, eventually entering a smaller field with a farmhouse visible on the far side. Follow it round, keeping right, and go through a kissing gate. Walk for a few paces towards a white gate, then duck left through a hole in the hedge out onto the road, beside the entrance to Parkfield Latimer. Turn right and follow the road (Church Lane) downhill, passing the Old Rectory on your left. Continue downhill to the church.

❺ Just beyond the church is the entrance to Latimer Place; take the tarmac drive running downhill to a weir. Enjoy superb views across the valley and back up the hill to Latimer Place. When the drive forks left and right, go straight on through the kissing gate and cross the pasture to the road via a kissing gate.

❻ Cross over to a kissing gate and follow the wide path half right up the sloping field towards woodland. Bear right to pass through a kissing gate, and about 75yds (69m) beyond it, veer left and climb steeply between the trees. Cross a wide track and head for a house. Keep to the right of it and join a drive leading to a road. Follow Chenies Avenue, cross Elizabeth Avenue and head down to a junction. Turn left and walk to Chalfont and Latimer Station to catch the train back to Chesham.

WHERE TO EAT AND DRINK There are no refreshment options on the rural stretches of the walk, but Chesham offers plenty of choice within easy walking distance of the station; the Queens Head is the best pub option.

WHAT TO SEE During World War II, Latimer Place (now a conference centre) housed important German prisoners of war – who were permitted servants, fine dining and even wine. In fact they were being secretly bugged by British Intelligence Services, using hidden listening devices. It is said that the information gleaned was of such magnitude that the project was given an unlimited budget by the Government.

From Chalfont St Giles to Jordans

DISTANCE 6.75 miles (10.9km)	**MINIMUM TIME** 2hrs 45min	

ASCENT/GRADIENT 98ft (30m) ▲▲▲   **LEVEL OF DIFFICULTY** +++

PATHS Paths across farmland and some road walking; several stiles

LANDSCAPE Undulating farmland and woodland on edge of the Chilterns

SUGGESTED MAP AA Leisure Map 17 The Chilterns

START/FINISH Grid reference: SU991937

DOG FRIENDLINESS On lead where signs request it and at Jordans

PARKING Car park off main street, almost opposite church

PUBLIC TOILETS In main street, near Milton's Cottage

A simple stone in a quiet burial ground in the Chilterns marks the grave of outspoken Quaker William Penn (1644–1718). There is nothing here that indicates what this man achieved in his lifetime – notably the founding of Pennsylvania in 1682 – for he died in poverty and abject circumstances. Penn had a difficult life. Imprisoned several times for speaking out against religious principles, he always remained loyal to his beliefs, but struggled with business details. It was Penn who secured the release, in 1686, of almost 2,000 people imprisoned on religious grounds. William and his wives, Gulielma and Hannah, together with 10 of their 16 children, are interred in the burial ground beside the historic Meeting House. This had been built by Quakers in 1688 as soon as the Declaration of Indulgence, issued by James II, ended the persecution of Nonconformists. Step inside – looking at the plain wooden benches and the walls decorated with portraits, it is as if time has stood still.

JORDANS FARM

During the 17th century Old Jordans Farm, next door to the Meeting House, was a meeting place of the early pioneering Quakers, as well as the scene of religious persecution. William Penn worshipped here with fellow Quakers, but meetings were frequently broken up by order of the local court. Undeterred, these people continued to spread their message, often travelling to the far-flung corners of the country.

Old Jordans remained in Quaker hands until the early years of the 18th century. In 1910 the Society of Friends discovered that the farm, now virtually derelict, was up for sale. They acquired it, with members adding a wing in 1920. Old Jordans served for many years as a Quaker guest house and conference centre, but is now closed. It used to attract visitors from all over the world, and was described as a 'well where men come to draw waters of peace'.

MAYFLOWER TIMBERS

On the south side of the garden lies the Mayflower Barn, originally the main barn of Old Jordans farm and named after the vessel which carried the Pilgrim Fathers to America in 1620. The barn, built in the same year that the *Mayflower* was broken up, is said to contain timber from the ship.

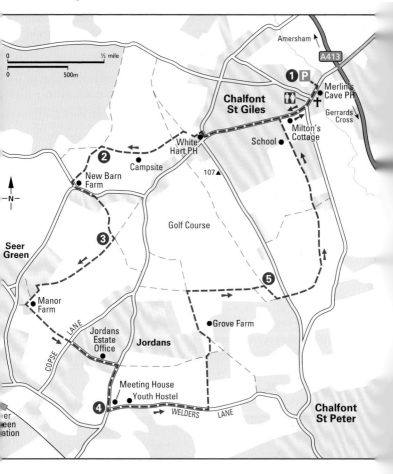

1 Turn right out of the car park and walk through the village, passing Milton's Cottage. At the White Hart turn right into Back Lane, swinging left after 55yds (50m) onto a footpath at a sharp bend. Follow the path around the field and through a kissing gate. Take the left fork, continue past a kissing gate and a stile to a staggered wooden fence straight ahead. Shortly after, where

the footpath and bridleway meet, bear left then immediately right, to continue straight on the other side of the hedge. Ignore the large gate; instead, pass an old stile and, keeping close to the hedge, walk straight ahead to another disused stile. Carry on past a campsite to the corner of the field. Instead of going left past the campsite, go straight through another gap in the hedge. Cut diagonally across the corner of this next field, over a grassy track, to an overgrown and indistinct gap in the hedge ahead. Through the gap, take the waymarked path half right across a paddock, through three gates, to a disused stile in the line of trees.

2 Turn left and follow a woodland trail for some 325yds (297m) to New Barn Farm, crossing a stile about halfway along. At the road turn left, and go left again at the junction. Just beyond a left bend, turn right along the poorly waymarked drive to Willow Court Stables. Go through a kissing gate and follow the fenced path beside paddocks.

3 On reaching a crossroads, turn right through a kissing gate and walk under power lines. At the metal gate skirt round the edge of the recreation ground to the red dog-waste bin. Follow the waymarked path around the field and on to a junction at Manor Farm. Cross the drive onto the wide, tree-lined path opposite. At the bottom of the hill go straight across the junction and up between houses. Cross Copse Lane and continue past Jordans recreation ground to a T-junction. Turn right on the road towards Seer Green, past the Mayflower Barn. Just before a 40mph sign, bear left through a kissing gate and take the path down to the graveyard and Meeting House. A gate in the far right-hand corner of the graveyard brings you back to the road.

4 Turn left almost immediately into Welders Lane, initially walking uphill past the entrance to Jordans Youth Hostel. After 0.5 miles (800m) turn left onto a track signposted 'Lazdon Farm' and 'Grove Farm'; follow this to the second kissing gate on the left. Head diagonally across a paddock, passing beneath power lines, with stables right. Walk parallel to the power lines and go through four kissing gates to a stile. Turn right and follow the fenced path to a kissing gate. Keep straight along the path, past a public footpath to the right, as far as a T-junction of paths.

5 Swing right, pass through the trees and bear left at another junction to a kissing gate by the road. Cross over and follow an enclosed path. Eventually you'll come to a track between two houses. Cross over, go through a gate, and – keeping to the hedge – continue straight down the field and then up, past a bowling green, playing fields and a recreation ground. In the far right-hand corner of the last field turn right. Follow the path as it skirts round a playground and down to the road at the Milton's Head. Turn right and retrace your steps to the car park.

WHERE TO EAT AND DRINK The Merlin's Cave in Chalfont St Giles offers the usual pub favourites at reasonable prices. The Deli, a few doors along, serves top-quality sandwiches, wraps and pastries as well as hearty breakfasts.

WHAT TO SEE The estate office at Jordans recalls the life and work of Fred Hancock, secretary of the village for 25 years. A plaque describes his achievements, and how he devoted himself to the maintenance and welfare of the village.

WHILE YOU'RE THERE John Milton (1608–74), one of England's greatest poets, settled in Chalfont St Giles in 1665, fleeing the plague in London to finish *Paradise Lost* (1665). Today his home and garden are open to the public. The village doubled as Walmington-on-Sea in the film version of *Dad's Army* (1971).

West Wycombe and Hughenden Manor

DISTANCE 7 miles (11.3km)   MINIMUM TIME 2hrs 45min

ASCENT/GRADIENT 280ft (85m) ▲▲▲   LEVEL OF DIFFICULTY ✦✦✦

PATHS Field, woodland and parkland paths, some roads

LANDSCAPE Heart of Chilterns, north of High Wycombe

SUGGESTED MAP AA Walker's Map 24 The Chilterns

START/FINISH Grid reference: SU827950

DOG FRIENDLINESS Lead required in villages; signs at various points request dogs be on lead or under control

PARKING Car park by church and mausoleum at West Wycombe

PUBLIC TOILETS Hughenden Manor, West Wycombe House

Looking at Hughenden Manor's delightful setting on the slope of a hill and surrounded by woods and unspoiled parkland, it's not difficult to see why Benjamin Disraeli, Queen Victoria's favourite prime minister, chose it as his country home in 1848.

Born in 1804, the baptised son of a Spanish Jew, Disraeli was clever and ambitious. Fiercely political, his main objectives in life were to further the cause of the workers, popularise the monarchy and foster the might, unity and glory of the British Empire. His greatest political rival was the Liberal leader William Gladstone, who disliked Disraeli's imperialism and his grand notions of empire.

QUEEN'S FAVOURITE

It was Disraeli who turned Queen Victoria against Gladstone, forging a close association with the monarch at a time when she most needed the trust and support of others. After her beloved Albert died in 1861, Victoria withdrew from public life to mourn his loss. As the years passed, she became an increasingly distant and reclusive figure – isolated from her family and her subjects. Benjamin Disraeli coaxed her back, winning her trust and giving her the confidence she needed to continue as queen. Towards the end of his life he became one of her closest confidants.

By the time he moved with his wife, Mary Ann Lewis, to Hughenden, Disraeli was an established novelist as well as a significant figure in British politics. As leader of the Conservative Party in the House of Commons, it was clear he was destined for higher office. Disraeli became Chancellor of the Exchequer in Lord Derby's three successive ministries and Prime Minister in the 1860s and 1870s. Widowed in

1872, he was created Earl of Beaconsfield four years later, remaining at Hughenden until he died in 1881.

When Disraeli purchased Hughenden Manor it was a white-painted, three-storeyed Georgian building of simple, unfussy design. The house was given a Gothic flavour by the architect E B Lamb in 1862, and the west wing was added by Disraeli's nephew, Coningsby. Now in the care of the National Trust, Hughenden contains most of Disraeli's books, pictures and furniture. There are manuscripts and letters from Queen Victoria, who spent some time in Disraeli's study after his funeral. The display case in the Disraeli Room has a copy of Prince Albert's speeches and addresses, given by Queen Victoria in gratitude for his moving speech in the House of Commons following the Prince Consort's death.

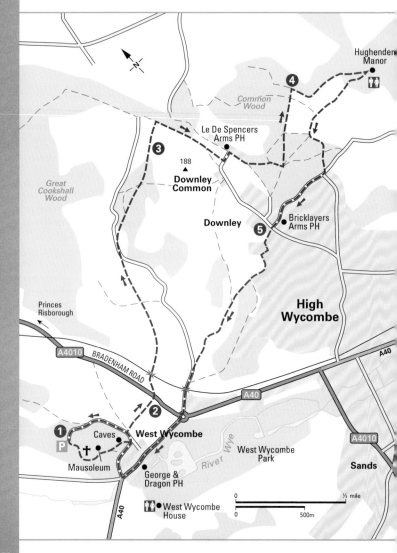

1 From the car park, enter the churchyard and pass to the immediate right of the church. Skirting the wall, continue on the path to the mausoleum, then line up with the A40 towards High Wycombe. Take the grassy path down the hillside (not the path on the right) to steps. Descend to the road, emerging by the Hell-Fire Caves. Turn left along the road, pass a 'Church Lane' sign, and take the next path right, via a kissing gate. Keeping to the right-hand boundary of the field, look for another kissing gate, then cross into the adjoining field, and go straight ahead down to a further kissing gate by the road.

2 Cross over, make for the trees, pass under the railway and over a stile. At the field go straight ahead, keeping to the right of the fence. Follow the path across a track, through a willow copse, and down to a second track. Continue up the field opposite towards a converted barn. With the hedge left, bear left onto a lane. At the bottom of the hill, swing right at the waymarker and follow the ride through woodland. Eventually reach a kissing gate, beyond which the path leads through a field.

3 Cross the field and go through a kissing gate to a track. Turn right and cut straight through the wood, ignoring turnings. Emerge at a cricket pitch and bear left along the road to a corner. Turn left for the Le De Spencers Arms or, to continue the walk, turn right past houses. When the track bends sharply left around the houses, bear right across the common and shortly into a wood. At the bottom of the hill, by a NT sign, turn sharp left (not along the bridleway). Follow the path (marked by white arrows) straight through the woods down to a crossroads. Take the path straight ahead up the steep slope to a T-junction.

4 Turn right and follow this path round fields and through woodland to a crossing point. Swing left along the bridleway to Hughenden Manor, or right to continue. Follow the track down, then alongside fields, and make for tree cover. Entering the wood, bear left up the slope through the trees, following the odd white arrow. Emerge between the Scout hut and a house and turn right onto Coates Lane. Pass the Bricklayers Arms and go straight over at the junction onto a footpath.

5 Keep ahead on either path through the trees to a housing estate. Pass the school, then turn immediately right to follow a footpath as it skirts round the school and runs down to a junction. Head straight across through trees to a sunken path, past a galvanised gate, and on to a T-junction. Bear left downhill to a lane, then left again. Follow this under a railway to a road by a garage. Cross Bradenham Road, turn right at the roundabout and walk into West Wycombe. At the end of the village turn sharp right into Church Lane and return to the car park.

WHERE TO EAT AND DRINK There is a cafe at West Wycombe's Hell-Fire Caves. Further on is the Le De Spencers Arms at Downley, offering home-cooked pub meals. The Bricklayers Arms, also at Downley, serves high-quality dishes.

WHILE YOU'RE THERE Visit West Wycombe House, built in the 18th century for Sir Francis Dashwood, founder of the Dilettanti Society and the notorious Hellfire Club. The Italianate house is famous for its rococo garden.

Turville and Fingest

DISTANCE 3 miles (4.8km)   MINIMUM TIME 1hr 30min

ASCENT/GRADIENT 150ft (46m) ▲▲▲   LEVEL OF DIFFICULTY ✦✦✦

PATHS Field and woodland paths, some road walking

LANDSCAPE Rolling Chiltern countryside, farmland and woodland

SUGGESTED MAP AA Walker's Map 24 The Chilterns

START/FINISH Grid reference: SU767911

DOG FRIENDLINESS Lead required in villages and across farmland

PARKING Small parking area in centre of Turville

PUBLIC TOILETS None on route

A visit to the delightful Chiltern village of Turville leaves you with the impression that you may have been here before – not in reality perhaps, but in the private world of fantasy and imagination. It's more than likely you have been to Turville without ever leaving your armchair, for Turville is one of Britain's most frequently used film and television locations. Its picturesque cottages and secluded setting at the bottom of a remote valley make it an obvious choice for movie-makers and production companies.

Over the years the village has featured regularly both on the large and small screen. Two notable productions brought Turville to the attention of television audiences in the 1990s. The BBC comedy *The Vicar of Dibley*, starring Dawn French in the title role, was partly filmed in the village, and the tiny cottage by the entrance to the church doubled as the vicar's home. In 1998, the village was extensively used in the award-winning ITV drama *Goodnight Mister Tom*, with the late John Thaw. This delightful wartime story was an immediate hit and Turville's classic village 'Englishness' was the programme's cornerstone.

Goodnight Mister Tom may have been set during World War II, but one of Britain's most famous propaganda movies was actually shot here during wartime. *Went the Day Well?*, based on a short story by Grahame Greene, dates back to 1942, and tells how a small English village responded to capture by German fifth columnists. Several locals and ex-residents of Turville recall how they moved props on a handcart and pushed rolls of barbed wire on cartwheels, which were used in the film as blockades. The Old School House, by the green, was the local police station in the story.

Overlooking the village is Cobstone Mill, an 18th-century smock mill, which has also played a key part in various productions. The windmill was used in a 1976 episode of *The New Avengers* television series in which Purdey and Gambit, played by Joanna Lumley and Gareth Hunt, drove through the village in a yellow MGB, chasing a helicopter that landed by the windmill. Cobstone Mill was also used in the children's film classic *Chitty Chitty Bang Bang* (1968), starring Dick Van Dyke as Caractacus Potts, who transforms an old racing car into a wondrous flying toy. In the movie, the family lived in the windmill.

And so it continues – in spring 2013 George Clooney and Matt Damon were in nearby Fingest working on a new film, *The Monuments Men*, a World War II drama released in 2014.

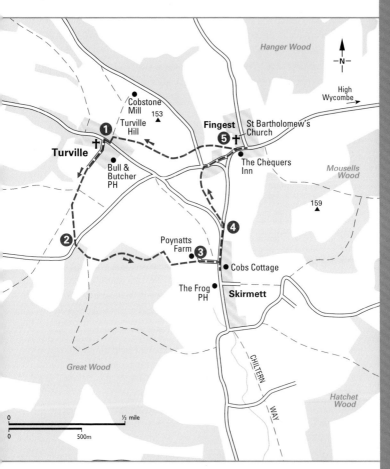

❶ Take the lane to the left of the church entrance by the old School (children playing) sign, with Sleepy Cottage on the corner. Pass Square Close Cottages and the village school before continuing on the Chiltern Way through a tunnel of trees. Climb gently to a gate and keep ahead along the field edge to a waymarker in the boundary. Branch

left at this point through a path bisecting the field and head diagonally down the field to a gate.

❷ Cross the road to another gate and follow the track through the trees, passing a gas installation on the right. After a few yards you will break cover from the trees. Ignore the broad grassy path branching off to the right and continue up the field slope to the next belt of trees. Turville and the windmill are clearly seen over to the left. Enter the woodland and keep left at the junction. Follow the clear, wide path as it contours round the slopes, dotted with beech trees to the left. Descend the hillside, keeping to the woodland edge. Follow the fence around to the right. As you descend, Skirmett comes into view down below to your left. Bear left at the next corner, heading to a gate by Poynatts Farm.

❸ Walk along the drive to the road, bear right and enter Skirmett. Directly opposite you is a row of picture-postcard cottages including Cobs Cottage and Ramblers. Go left out of the village, passing All Saints, Skirmett Gospel Mission Hall and The Chapel House, all now private houses.

❹ Just past the junction with flooded Watery Lane, go through the gate immediately to the right of this lane cum-stream. Go through two fields, each of which are gated, and exit at a third gate. Turn right into Fingest village. Bear left at the main road by Fingest House, and follow its flint wall round to the left to find the waymarked Chiltern Way footpath leading back to Turville. Before leaving the village, visit the early Norman church of St Bartholomew's. It has an unusual tower, with a double vaulted roof.

❺ The flint wall of Fingest House gives way to a hedge, then field. At the waymarked junction at the corner of the field turn left, go through a gate and follow the path between trees, offering a teasing glimpse of the Chiltern Hills. Go through a kissing gate and head diagonally down the field, enjoying the rooftop views of Turville. Look above you to the right to see the famous windmill. Follow the track back to the village green.

WHERE TO EAT AND DRINK There are several excellent pubs along the way. Both the Bull and Butcher at Turville and The Chequers Inn, opposite the church at Fingest, offer a superior line in pub food, while The Frog at Skirmett is a gastropub with reasonably priced baguettes at lunchtime.

WHAT TO SEE Some of the best views of the Chilterns can be enjoyed on this scenic walk. The chalk hills are thick with beech woods, which makes walking here a joy at any time of the year.

WHILE YOU'RE THERE There has been a church on the same site in Turville for over 800 years. The oldest part of the present church is the nave, which dates back to the early 12th century; the squat tower is 14th century. Do look inside at its ornate memorials. Fans of *The Vicar of Dibley* may recognize it as the 'Church of St Barnabus' (named after St Barnabus of Wolverhampton!).

Hambleden and the Chiltern Way

DISTANCE 5.5 miles (8.8km)	**MINIMUM TIME** 2hrs 15min

ASCENT/GRADIENT 215ft (65m) ▲▲▲   **LEVEL OF DIFFICULTY** +++

PATHS Field and woodland paths, some road walking

LANDSCAPE Rolling Chiltern countryside, farmland and woodland

SUGGESTED MAP AA Walker's Map 24 The Chilterns

START/FINISH Grid reference: SU785865

DOG FRIENDLINESS Lead required across farmland

PARKING Public car park behind the Stag and Huntsman (signposted)

PUBLIC TOILETS None on route

The centre of this beautiful little village, happily bypassed by traffic, features picture-postcard, flint-faced terraced cottages, and a quaint trough and water pump. It is in the care of a private estate and under the protection of The National Trust, so little happens here without very careful consideration, and there have been few changes over the last century. A prime example is the old iron water pump in the centre, which until 1956 provided the village's main water supply. In 2013 Hambleden was ranked one of the 30 Best Villages in Britain by *The Times*.

LOCATION LOCATION LOCATION

Because it is so little altered, like neighbouring Turville (see Walk 19), picturesque Hambleden is a favourite location for film and television crews. Major films shot here include *Chitty Chitty Bang Bang, The Witches, Dance with a Stranger, The Avengers* (1998 version), *101 Dalmatians* and *Sleepy Hollow*. Many episodes – including the very first – of *Midsomer Murders* were filmed here, while in *Band of Brothers* Hambleden was Easy Company's training base in England.

FAMOUS NAMES

The village boasts two famous residents. The first was Major General James Thomas Brudenell, born at the Manor House in 1797. Better known as Lord Cardigan, he led the ill-fated Charge of the Light Brigade in 1854, resulting in 156 men dead or missing, a further 127 wounded and 60 taken prisoner. Despite the fact that he bravely led the charge from the front, Lord Cardigan survived the carnage, and the extent to which he was to blame for it all is unproven. Whatever the truth of the matter, he was a man of considerable style and coolness; it is said that after reaching the Russian guns and having taken part in the fighting, he rode back up 'the valley of death', saw that nothing more could be done that day, and so retired to his yacht in Balaclava harbour and took dinner with champagne.

Less dramatically, William Henry Smith (1792–1865) lived in the village. He built his family company into Britain's leading newsagent, named from his initials, W H Smith. You can find a memorial to him in the churchyard.

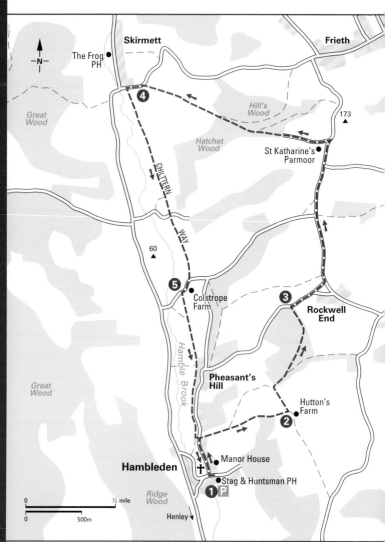

① Before setting off, spend a little time looking around the tiny centre of the village. Walk back towards the car park, turn left opposite the pub and continue along the main road, after a

few paces passing the grand Manor House of 1603. Turn right up a lane to Hutton's Farm, and continue straight ahead past an intercom point with rising bollards. Follow it up and up, through the trees, ignoring all turns off here, until you reach the entrance to Hutton's Farm, to your right.

2 Turn left, enjoying the panoramic views, and go through a gate beside a fenced-off field. Follow the dirt track into woodland. Keep left at a waymarked fork, cross a track and continue ahead on the path. Cross a stile and keep right at the road.

3 You are now at Rockwell End, with little to distinguish it in the way of landmarks (though episodes of *Midsomer Murders* have been shot here). Continue to follow the road round to the left. This is a long stretch of road walking, but traffic is generally very light. After around 0.75 miles (1.2km) you will see a large house, St Katharine's Parmoor. Continue a few paces beyond here and turn left, following the lane, which is tarmac as far as a house with balcony. It dwindles to a path at this point and descends gradually between trees and bushes with fine views between hedges to the left. Pass a path running off sharp right, and then another, before descending between hedges to the road.

4 Turn left, then take the next waymarker left onto the Chiltern Way footpath. This cuts straight ahead across fields for around 1 mile (1.6km). Cross a lane and keep to the left of the house, following the path through the trees. Keep alongside a hedge, heading towards houses. Cross the field and continue on a track. Go straight on at the road, passing Colstrope Farm on the left. Look for a kissing gate on the right-hand bend.

5 Continue ahead to a kissing gate and keep the field-edge on your right. Head for a kissing gate and continue, with the field-edge now on your left. Make for Pheasant's Hill through two kissing gates. Cross a drive to a further kissing gate and continue beside a paddock. Pass through two kissing gates, either side of a conifer belt, and cross the next field with a fence on your right. Go through a kissing gate and veer left to another. As Hambleden Church draws close, cross the last field diagonally right to emerge by a small bridge. Follow the road back into the village to return to the car park, passing a clear, babbling stream to your right.

WHERE TO EAT AND DRINK The Stag and Huntsman serves up superior pub favourites with the emphasis on local and estate produce, and with a large variety of game when in season. The village post office doubles as a simple cafe, with outdoor benches, and also sells picnic supplies.

WHAT TO SEE St Katharine's Parmoor, formerly a convent dating from the mid-14th century, is now a house of retreat. The lands once belonged to the Knights Templar, and the cedar tree here is said to have been grown from a seed from the Lebanon, collected during the Crusades. Sir Stafford Cripps, the post-war Chancellor of the Exchequer, was born here, and during World War II it was home to the exiled King Zog of Albania.

WHILE YOU'RE THERE Don't miss a visit to the beautiful 12th-century Church of St Mary the Virgin in Hambledon. Beside its entrance, Lychgate Cottage displays an original 17th-century royal fire plaque. These were used before the days of public fire brigades to denote which houses had fire insurance – only houses with the correct plaque would be extinguished by private companies in case of a blaze.

The meandering Thames at Marlow

DISTANCE 4 miles (6.4km)   MINIMUM TIME 1hr 30min

ASCENT/GRADIENT Negligible ▲ ▲ ▲   LEVEL OF DIFFICULTY ✚ ✚ ✚

PATHS Pavements, paved paths, lane and byway, field and meadow paths, tow path

LANDSCAPE Thames Valley townscape and meadows

SUGGESTED MAP AA Walker's Map 24 The Chilterns

START/FINISH Grid reference: SU849865

DOG FRIENDLINESS Lead required in Marlow; under strict control on Thames Path

PARKING Car parks in Pound Lane and Oxford Road, off West Street

PUBLIC TOILETS Behind Waitrose at river end of High Street; Higginson Park

A stroll through the streets of this charming, well-to-do Thameside town reveals many buildings and places of architectural, historic and literary interest. Jerome K Jerome, T S Eliot and both Percy and Mary Shelley all took inspiration while staying here. In fact they were all just a few yards away from each other, albeit at different times.

In 1817, what is now Shelley House and Shelley Lodge on West Street was the home of the poet Percy Bysshe Shelley and his novelist wife Mary Wollstonecraft Godwin. While Percy was out boating on the river, writing much of *The Revolt of Islam* (1818), Mary would be at home working on her classic novel *Frankenstein* (1818). From here the couple moved to Italy.

Later came Jerome K Jerome, who stayed at the Crown Hotel, at the junction of West Street and High Street, while writing *Three Men in a Boat* (1889). A few paces away, and some 28 years later, No. 31 West Street was the home of T S Eliot between 1917 and 1920. This was the period when his first important poetry, most famously *Prufrock and Other Observations* (1917), was widely published. Considered shocking and offensive in its own day, *Prufrock* is now regarded as being one of the first Modernist works of poetry.

Marlow is of course inextricably linked with the Thames, and in Marlow Bridge, linking Buckinghamshire and Berkshire, it boasts one of the most striking crossings on the entire river. This was completed in 1832 by William Tierney Clark, who had previously designed the suspension bridge at Hammersmith (since replaced) and the landmark Széchenyi Chain suspension bridge across the Danube in Budapest. The Marlow and Budapest bridges are now the only surviving examples of his work.

Marlow Bridge makes a wonderful backdrop to the annual Marlow Regatta, which used to finish close to here. In fact, somewhat confusingly, the Marlow Town Regatta still does, but the internationally acclaimed Marlow Regatta event moved in 2001, after 145 years on the Thames, to the multi-lane rowing course at Dorney Lake. Marlow's most famous current resident, Sir Steven Redgrave, five times Olympic rowing champion, is immortalized in bronze in the riverside park, looking across the Thames towards the regatta finishing post.

Just across the other side of the bridge is the Compleat Angler, one of the South's most famous hotels. Omar Sharif, Clint Eastwood and Naomi Campbell are among many celebrities who have stayed at the hotel over the years, and in 1999 it claimed to have become the first public restaurant outside London to be visited by the Queen for a meal.

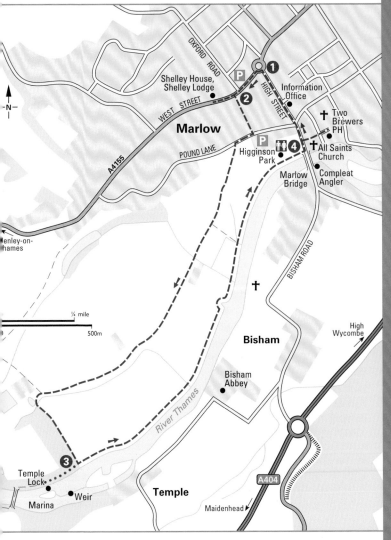

1 Make for the junction at the top of the High Street, where an obelisk commemorates the Hatfield–Bath turnpike road. The impressive building now occupied by Steamer Trading Cook Shop was built in 1806 as the town hall. It subsequently served as a covered market, fire station, assembly rooms and town prison – the cell can still be seen on the ground floor. The building was also part of the Crown Hotel. Facing the shop, turn left into West Street. Go past No. 31, noting the blue plaque to T S Eliot, and pass Ye Olde Tuck Shoppe (right) to see Shelley House and Shelley Lodge. Retrace your steps, almost to the Thai Square restaurant, and turn right along Portlands Alley.

2 Follow the path, turn right at the next junction, then branch left into Lower Pound Lane, passing tennis courts on the right, and a cricket club, left. Continue ahead past the 'Private Road' sign. The long straight path heads through the trees, crosses a bridge and eventually dwindles to a narrow countryside path via a kissing gate. To your right are expansive views over fields and woods. Turn left at the T-junction (into Harleyford Lane) and this will shortly bring you to the Thames.

3 The walk heads left, downstream towards Marlow, but you may wish to make the short detour, upstream, to the weir to see the boats queue up to pass through pretty Temple Lock. Head back towards Marlow on the riverbank, and after a few hundred yards look across to the opposite bank to see the various buildings of Bisham Abbey edge into view. Continue ahead and eventually you will see Marlow's striking parish church and the suspension bridge. Just before the bridge the riverside path enters Higginson Park, with its playing fields, cafe and statue of Sir Steven Redgrave. Turn left at the bridge, back onto the High Street.

4 Follow the High Street, with Marlow's war memorial and the George and Dragon pub seen over on the right. To visit the Two Brewers pub, take the alleyway on the right, just beyond the church and bear right, to St Peter Street. Retrace your steps and turn right along the High Street. Just past Zizzi's, on the left-hand side, a narrow street leads to the site of the Thomas Wethered Brewery. It closed in 1987 but its buildings remain, now converted to other uses. Continue along the High Street to return to your car.

WHERE TO EAT AND DRINK Marlow caters for all tastes and budgets. The Two Brewers, a popular haunt of Jerome K Jerome, is a fine 18th-century watering hole towards the end of the walk. Higginson Park is perfect for a riverside picnic, and there is also a cafe here.

WHAT TO SEE Bisham Abbey, on the opposite bank of the Thames, presents a striking picture on the walk. The Tudor house was built by Sir Philip Hoby, Henry VIII's Ambassador to the Holy Roman Empire, using fragments of the original abbey. Its grounds are now part of the National Sports Centre, home to the England Hockey and GB Canoeing teams while also providing facilities for many other elite sportsmen and women.

WHILE YOU'RE THERE Rebuilt in 1835, All Saints Church occupies a delightful riverside setting at the bottom end of the High Street. There has been a church on this site since Saxon times, and inside are fascinating monuments.

A loop at Burnham Beeches

DISTANCE 4.5 miles (7.2km)   MINIMUM TIME 1hr 45min

ASCENT/GRADIENT 150ft (46m) ▲▲▲   LEVEL OF DIFFICULTY ✦✦✦

PATHS Woodland paths and drives, field paths, tracks and stretches of road; several stiles

LANDSCAPE Dense woodland and some open farmland between Slough and Beaconsfield

SUGGESTED MAP OS Explorer 172 Chiltern Hills East

START/FINISH Grid reference: SU957850

DOG FRIENDLINESS Keep under strict control

PARKING Car park at Burnham Beeches

PUBLIC TOILETS Burnham Beeches

Before the Corporation of the City of London bought Burnham Beeches in 1880 for public use and enjoyment, it was described as an area of 'woodland and waste'. Up until that time it had been owned by the Grenville family of Dropmore, and on the estate is East Burnham Cottage, where the dramatist Richard Sheridan (1751–1816) and his bride spent their honeymoon after they eloped in 1773. Here, he wrote to a friend, '...were I in a descriptive vein, I would draw you some of the prettiest scenes imaginable'. Later, in the 19th century, historian George Grote lived here, entertaining such luminaries as Chopin, Mendelssohn, John Stuart Mill and singer Jenny Lind. It is fascinating to picture these individuals strolling among the beeches and admiring their beauty.

ANCIENT WOODLAND

Extending to 600 acres (243ha) and now a National Nature Reserve, Burnham Beeches contains the world's largest collection of ancient beeches, with an average age of more than 300 years. On the first part of the walk in particular keep an eye open for some of the oldest, gnarliest trees in all the forest. Many are well over 300 years old and could come straight out of the pages of a Grimm Brothers fairytale.

The steward of the Hundred of Burnham – one of the original Chiltern Hundreds, or Saxon administrative divisions – had an almost impossible job on his hands preventing highway robbery in and around these thick woodlands. The locals were very protective towards the beeches, treating them almost as if they were their own. When the corporation acquired Burnham Beeches, some people protested against the new bylaws in the strongest terms, attacking the keeper and throwing him into a pond.

Burnham Beeches was part of a huge forest that stretched across the Chilterns in prehistoric times. Much of that woodland has disappeared over the years, but the beeches at Burnham continue to remind us of that once thickly wooded landscape. The beech is one of Britain's most prolific trees and the county of Buckinghamshire is closely associated with what was once nicknamed 'the Chiltern weed'. Native to southern England, the beech has shallow, expanding roots allowing it to thrive on thin soil where many other trees will not grow. Its thick foliage permits only a hint of sunlight to reach the ground beneath it, discouraging the growth of other plants. As a result, a classic beech wood has a floor thickly strewn with its own deep brown, perfectly sculpted leaves.

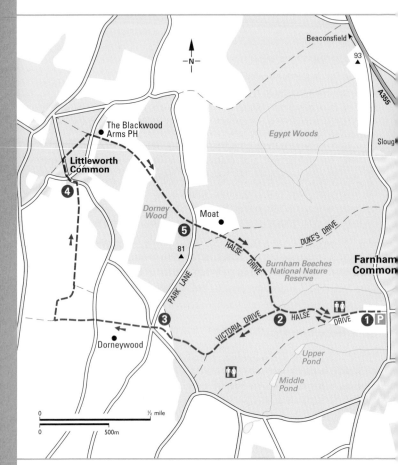

1 Follow the drive away from Farnham Common, keeping the car parking area on the left. Pass a refreshment kiosk and veer right at the fork just beyond it. Soon reach a gate where you enter the National Nature Reserve's car-free zone. Follow Halse Drive as it curves left and down between trees. At the bottom of the hill swing left into Victoria Drive.

2 Follow the broad, stony drive between the beeches, avoiding turnings either side of the route, and eventually reach a major junction with a wide path on the left and right. On the right is a large beech tree with 'Randy 6.9.97' carved on the trunk. If you manage to miss the path, you will soon reach the road. Bear right and go up the slope, keep left at the fork and cross several clearings to reach the road at the junction with Green Lane and Park Lane.

3 Cross the road to a stile and waymarker and go straight ahead, the boundary on your left. Make for a stile and descend into the field dip, quickly climbing again to pass alongside the grounds of Dorneywood. Walk ahead to the field corner, cross a stile and turn right at the road. Head for a waymarked footpath on the left and cross the field, with the hedge on your left, to a gap in the trees and hedgerow. Through the hedge, turn right and skirt three fields, with a large mansion on the hill to the left. The path cuts between two oak trees in the next field before reaching a gap in the hedgerow.

4 Turn left out to the road. Pass Common Lane and Horseshoe Hill (a blackboard sign points to the Blackwood Arms) and turn right at the next bridleway. Follow the track through the wood to the next road at Littleworth Common. Go through a kissing gate to the right of the Blackwood Arms and follow the Beeches Way. Beyond a gate continue ahead between the wood and a wire fence and through a kissing gate before following a fenced path. Go through a kissing gate and take the path between the trees of Dorney Wood, entering the Portman Burtley Estate.

5 On reaching a kissing gate, cross over to the road and continue ahead on the Beeches Way, past the junction of Morton Drive and McAuliffe Drive. Make for the next major intersection and keep right along Halse Drive. Pass Victoria Drive and retrace your steps back to the car park.

WHERE TO EAT AND DRINK There is a cafe at the car park where the walk starts and finishes. The Blackwood Arms at Littleworth Common serves a good range of high-quality bar food and real ales, and has a lovely garden.

WHAT TO SEE Dorneywood can be glimpsed from the path. This is the Chancellor of the Exchequer's official country residence, where pre-Budget meetings are held from time to time. The house was built in the 1920s.

WHILE YOU'RE THERE The grazing hardboard cow on the grass roof of the car park cafe was designed by a local 8-year-old schoolboy. While it's a bit of fun, it also has a serious point to make – grazing is the City Corporation's favoured grassland management technique as it is a traditional, environmentally friendly form of woodland management which provides a diverse range of grass heights.

Overleaf: Autumn at Burnham Beeches (Walk 22)

Stoke Poges and Stoke Green

DISTANCE 4 miles (6.4km) MINIMUM TIME 1hr 45min

ASCENT/GRADIENT Negligible ▲▲▲ LEVEL OF DIFFICULTY ✛✛✛

PATHS Semi-residential paths and drives, field tracks and paths, some road walking; many stiles

LANDSCAPE Partly residential, interspersed with golf courses

SUGGESTED MAP OS Explorer 172 Chiltern Hills East

START/FINISH Grid reference: SU977825

DOG FRIENDLINESS Lead required on golf courses, in Memorial Gardens and churchyard and in residential areas

PARKING Opposite Memorial Gardens; if gates locked, park in front of them

PUBLIC TOILETS Memorial Gardens, closed evenings and weekends

The walk starts at a beautiful Memorial Gardens – one of the few surviving gems of its kind, dating from the pre-war period. Still in use today, it makes for a perfect end to the walk, whether enjoying a picnic or simply resting your feet. The adjacent churchyard of St Giles is the very one which is said to have inspired poet Thomas Gray to write his famous 'Elegy Written in a Country Churchyard' (1751), one of the nation's favourite poems. Perhaps fittingly, Gray is buried here in the churchyard (beside his mother). In the adjacent field is a huge memorial, erected in 1799 by John Penn, grandson of William Penn (founder of Pennsylvania province). Lines from Gray's 'Elegy' are carved on the monument.

ETERNAL PEACE

The Memorial Gardens were founded in 1930 on land that formed part of Stoke Park. The aim was to provide a corner of peace and beauty in an increasingly hectic world, and today they remain a haven of tranquillity. The gardens were designed by one of the country's top landscape architects of the day, Sir Edward White. Dedicated in 1935 as non-denominational memorial grounds, they were acquired by the local authority in 1971and are registered as Grade II on the English Heritage Register of Parks and Gardens of special historic interest in England.

Those who loved the gardens in life often choose to have their ashes interred here, with small memorial plaques and flower holders commemorating them. The grounds cover 20 acres (8ha) with 2,000 private gardens, including rock and water gardens, rose gardens, parterre gardens, heath gardens and individual specimen trees and shrubs. There are also formal gardens enclosed by yew hedges, and informal gardens surrounded by glorious flowering shrubs. Running through the Memorial Gardens is the main avenue which leads down to the colonnade, characterised by columns, water channels, magnolia trees and bright flower beds. The park's tour de force, however, is its lake. Here a grassy slope tumbles down to the water and offers one of the finest views in all England.

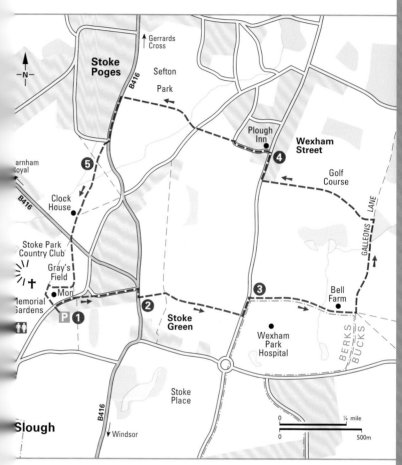

❶ From the car park, turn right and walk along the road. After a hundred yards (91m), cross over and look for a waymarker and a kissing gate by an oak on the right. Go through the gate and follow the path as it runs parallel at first with the road, and (rather disconcertingly) across the entrances to various houses. Go through two more kissing gates before the path joins a residential drive, Duffeld Park. Bear right when you get to the road junction, then take the first footpath left, by the sign for Snitterfeld House.

❷ Follow the wide tarmac drive, and opposite the entrance to Snitterfield House take a stile on the right. Go diagonally across a small field to a stile and bridge, and keep along the right-hand edge of the field. Look for a stile by an oak tree in the corner of the field, and go straight ahead across the next field, via another stile to the road. Turn left, passing hospital entrance gate No. 1. Immediately beyond it on the right is a barred metal gate (with private drive sign) and an electricity transformer. Beside the gate, to the right, is a public footpath sign and stile (possibly hidden by foliage). Wriggle through here and follow the track.

❸ After a few paces cross the next stile and continue ahead to Bell Farm. Pass the outbuildings and stables and keep ahead on a grassy track to a stile and gate. Cross a stile, turn left and follow a bridleway to a plank bridge and stile on the left. The walk now crosses a golf course. Cut across the fairway (following yellow marker posts) to a wide path, and follow it to the car park and club house. Take the drive leading out to the main road, veering right to a stile by a row of houses, and follow the track to the road. Bear right and walk along to the Plough Inn.

❹ Turn left into Plough Lane and when it bends right, go straight on along the public bridleway. Cross the next road to a kissing gate and continue on a waymarked path. Keep ahead, bearing left via two kissing gates to cross a small golf course, to reach a kissing gate leading out to the road. Turn left and walk along to Rogers Lane on the right. Make for the kissing gate on the corner and follow the outline of the path, running parallel to the road, ahead to a second gate.

❺ Through the gate, branch half right and follow the path through four more kissing gates (at the third you will see the Clock House) to reach the road. Cross over to a kissing gate and follow the straight path across Gray's Field towards the monument to Thomas Gray. Keep to the right of the monument and look for the kissing gate leading into the churchyard of St Giles. Turn left to return to the car park.

WHERE TO EAT AND DRINK The Plough on Wexham Street is a useful watering hole with a pleasant beer garden. Wexham Golf Club clubhouse is friendly and inclusive, for drinks and light refreshments. The Memorial Gardens make a perfect picnic spot.

WHAT TO SEE The Church of St Giles is usually open and inside you'll find evidence of Saxon, Norman, early Gothic and Tudor influences. At the western end of the church is what is known as the 'Bicycle Window', which depicts a naked cherub-like man sitting astride what appears to be some sort of ancient hobby-horse while blowing a horn. The stained glass dates from 1643.

WHILE YOU'RE THERE In the Memorial Gardens make for the lake and enjoy the magnificent view across the Palladian bridge to Stoke Park Country Club, Spa and Hotel. This is the focal point of a classical manicured landscape, designed by Lancelot 'Capability' Brown and Humphry Repton. The mansion was designed by James Wyatt (architect to George III) between 1790 and 1813. It has served as a shooting location for many famous films, including *Bridget Jones's Diary* (2001) and two of the *James Bond* movies.

Around the lake at Dorney

DISTANCE 5 miles (8km)	MINIMUM TIME 1hr 45min

ASCENT/GRADIENT Negligible ▲ ▲ ▲   LEVEL OF DIFFICULTY ✚ ✚ ✚

PATHS Roads, firm paths and Thames tow path

LANDSCAPE Lowland Thames valley

SUGGESTED MAP OS Explorer 160 Windsor, Weybridge & Bracknell

START/FINISH Grid reference: SU938776

DOG FRIENDLINESS Lead required in Dorney and by river

PARKING Car park at Dorney Common, tucked away off Boveney Road

PUBLIC TOILETS None on route

Located in Buckinghamshire's most southerly village, close to the Thames, Dorney Court is a genuine medieval village manor house – its jumble of timber-framed gables has survived intact and unchanged for some 600 years, looking much the same today as when it was first built. Back in the mid-1920s, *Country Life* magazine described Dorney Court as 'one of the finest Tudor manor houses in England'. Few would dispute that label and what endears the house to so many people is its long tradition of continuous family occupation – more than 450 years.

The first owner was recorded after the Norman Conquest, and after changing hands several times in the 15th century the house was sold in 1504 for 500 marks. By the middle of the 16th century the manor, together with 600 acres (243ha), was owned by Sir William Garrard, Lord Mayor of London. It is through this family that the town of Gerrards Cross got its name. Sir William Garrard's daughter Martha married Sir James Palmer of Kent, and Dorney Court has remained in the Palmer family to this day. One family portrait depicts Jane Palmer, born in 1564 and a forebear of the late Diana, Princess of Wales. The layout of the house has changed little, and in recent years has been a film and television location setting for many period productions, including episodes of *Cranford, Poirot, Midsomer Murders, Elizabeth: the Golden Age* and many more.

FRUIT AND HONEY

The village of Dorney stands on a gentle rise in the Thames flood plain, and is cut off from the river by spacious meadows where evidence of prehistoric life can be found. The name Dorney means 'island of bumblebees' and the local Dorney honey is renowned for its delicate, light flavours.

The large carved stone pineapple standing in the corner of the Great Hall at Dorney Court commemorates the first pineapple to be grown in England. The story goes that the top of a pineapple, imported from Barbados, was sliced off at a dinner in London and given to the Earl of Castlemaine's gardener to plant at Dorney Court. The pineapple thrived, and was subsequently presented to Charles II in 1661.

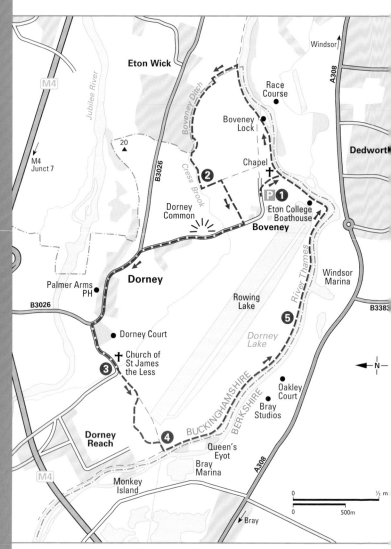

1 Exit the rear of the car park and turn right to the Chapel of St Mary Magdalen. Walk in front of the chapel, then turn left and continue downstream along the Thames Path, heading for Boveney Lock. Windsor Racecourse

can be seen over on the Berkshire bank. Continue on the tow path, cross Boveney Ditch on a footbridge and bear immediately left at a path junction. After 50 paces turn left over the footbridge, by the Sustrans milepost, and veer immediately right on a narrow dirt path. Skirt round the field, keeping the ditch hard by you on the right, and pass a row of houses on the far bank.

2 Bear left following the perimeter. Look for a waymarked footpath sign ahead (it may be partially hidden in a copse) and turn right to follow it between fields to a stile, back to Boveney Road. Turn right to follow the road across Dorney Common, towards Dorney village. Pass Wakehams, a timber-framed house with a well at the front. Away to the right is a fine view of Windsor Castle. Keep left at the T-junction, cross a cattle grid and join the pavement. Walk through Dorney, keeping the Palmer Arms on your right. Bear left into Court Lane, follow the path parallel to the road and pass the entrance to Dorney Court to reach the Church of St James the Less.

3 Continue on the path now on the left side of the lane, and when the road bends right, go straight ahead at the sign for Eton College Rowing Centre. Keep to the right-hand side of the drive and follow the path round to the right, by the low-level wooden waymarker, signed towards Maidenhead. The trail becomes the broad gravel Barge Path, popular with serious cyclists, so be alert. This leads to the Thames Path.

4 Turn left here and follow the river, facing Bray Marina on the opposite bank. Further downstream the imposing cream facade of Bray film studios edges into view, with its sweeping riverside lawns and weeping willows. Continue on the leafy Thames Path and you will soon catch sight of Oakley Court across the water on the opposite (Berkshire) bank of the river.

5 Beyond Oakley Court you'll see the cabin cruisers and gin palaces of Windsor Marina, and next to it lines of caravans and mobile homes overlooking the river. Through the trees on the Buckinghamshire bank is the outline of Eton College's new boathouse and its superb rowing lake, a star of the 2012 Olympics. To gain a closer view, briefly follow a path beside the river boathouse and slipway, go through a gate and walk towards the lake; and then retrace your steps to the Thames Path. On the opposite bank of the river is Windsor Race Course Yacht Basin and ahead now is the Chapel of St Mary Magdalen. Follow the path alongside the chapel to a kissing gate, and about 50yds (46m) beyond it reach a lane. With the Old Place opposite and an avenue of chestnut trees on the right, turn left and return to the car park.

WHERE TO EAT AND DRINK Adjacent to Dorney Court is Dorney Court Kitchen Garden Centre. This is a wonderful place on a summer's day, with outdoor seating in a lovely garden centre next to a restored Walled Garden. Most of the food on the menu, from breakfasts through light lunches and afternoon teas, is grown here, and everything is home cooked. If you prefer a pub, the Palmer Arms in Dorney offers a gastropub menu.

WHAT TO SEE With its Victorian Gothic facade, Oakley Court was an obvious choice for Hammer horror film producers – especially as it lies next door to Bray Studios, home of Hammer. The house, now a hotel, has been used in various movie productions, including *The Curse of Frankenstein* (1957) and *The Rocky Horror Picture Show* (1975).

Around Eton and Windsor

DISTANCE 3.5 miles (5.7km)		MINIMUM TIME 1hr 15min	

ASCENT/GRADIENT Negligible ▲▲▲   LEVEL OF DIFFICULTY +++

PATHS Pavements, drive, tow path, path across meadows and playing fields

LANDSCAPE Lowland meadows and town outskirts in Thames Valley

SUGGESTED MAP OS Explorer 160 Windsor, Weybridge & Bracknell

START/FINISH Grid reference: SU968772

DOG FRIENDLINESS Lead required in town streets

PARKING Car park at Windsor and Eton Riverside Station

PUBLIC TOILETS At station

NOTES This walk links the stations of Windsor and Eton, and Datchett; the return is via the train.

With its legendary reputation and background, Eton College represents one of the great institutions of learning. On its famous playing fields, according to the Duke of Wellington, the Battle of Waterloo was won. Eton has produced 19 British prime ministers, including David Cameron, and princes William and Harry are also Old Etonians.

Founded in 1440 by Henry VI, Eton was modelled on Winchester College. Originally it accommodated 70 poor scholars who were educated free of charge and who would then go on to King's College, Cambridge, the following year. Today it is an exclusive school for approximately 1,300 boys between the ages of 13 and 18, all of whom are boarders. The boys of Eton College still wear black tailcoats, a tradition that dates back to mourning for George III, a favourite monarch of the school.

The highlight of a public tour is Eton College Chapel, built between 1449 and 1482, and similar in many ways to the chapel of King's College, Cambridge, which was also founded by Henry VI. Raised 13ft (4m) above ground, the college chapel is safe from flooding should the Thames ever burst its banks. The original plan included a chapel that would be more than twice the size of the finished building, but when Henry was deposed the College found itself in much reduced financial circumstances. The splendid vaulted ceiling and the impressive 15th-century wall-paintings are two of the college chapel's most distinguished features.

FIT FOR A QUEEN

No visit to Windsor and Eton would be complete without touring its mighty castle, one of the Queen's official residences (a huge standard flies from the battlements when she is at home here). Founded as a fortress by William the Conqueror, the castle has been substantially altered and extended over the centuries and its appearance today is much as it would have been in the 14th century. The dominant feature is its Round Tower, built by Henry II and visible for miles around. The most recent restoration and building work followed the much publicised fire in 1992.

The castle is open to the public, though the state apartments are closed when the Queen is in residence. A Changing of the Guard ceremony, similar to (though smaller than) the more famous ceremony at Buckingham Palace, takes place (weather permitting) at around 11am from Monday to Saturday, on alternate days from August to March and daily during April, May, June and July, but never on a Sunday. Aim to arrive near the castle gates from around 10.30am to secure a viewing point.

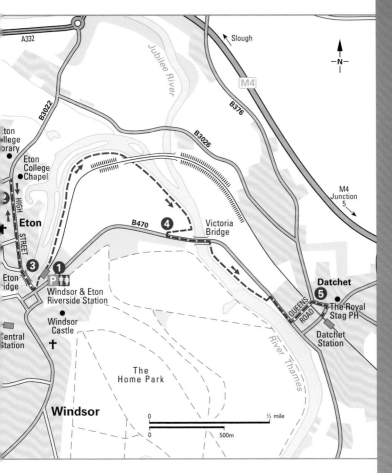

❶ From the railway station, turn right onto Farm Yard, left onto the river path, then right to cross Eton Bridge. Continue along the traffic-free High Street past individual shops and historic properties. The early-17th century Crown and Cushion, left, has been an inn since 1753. Right, at Nos. 47–49, the early-15th century building known as The Cockpit (now The Tiger Garden restaurant) is the oldest in Eton. Note the original fire plaque and stocks in front. The 1856 postbox was the first all-metal design and still functions today. At No. 98, on the left, The Turks Head is a former pub dating from c.1520.

2 Continue ahead, and at the end of the High Street are the buildings of Eton College. Right is the chapel; opposite is the entrance for public tours; beside it is the grand domed building housing the library. The ornate wrought-iron lamp here is known as 'The Burning Bush'. Return to the bridge.

3 Turn left onto Thames Side. Go through a set of wrought-iron gates and follow Romney Walk. There are good views from here to Windsor Castle to one side, while on the other bank – foliage permitting – you can catch glimpses of Eton College and the chapel. Continue ahead on a drive, pass a cottage dated 1898, and an octagonal building of 1912 which houses the waterworks for Windsor Castle. On reaching a boatyard, turn left to the water's edge and go through a kissing gate to walk along the grassy tow path beside the river. Pass under a railway bridge. Keep to the river path, but as you approach the next bridge veer right to the far end of the white railings.

4 Turn left and follow the pavement over Victoria Bridge. Bear right on the far side and follow the Thames Path through the trees, with views of the Thames and the Home Park and the pinnacles of the Chapel of St George, Windsor Castle. On reaching the road, via a footbridge, turn right along the B470, then left into Queens Road, and walk into the centre of Datchet.

5 This attractive riverside village has many historic buildings and strong literary associations. The main road to Windsor was the Datchet Lane in Shakespeare's *The Merry Wives of Windsor* (1602). Falstaff was transported along this road on his way to face a ducking in the Thames. The village is also mentioned in Jerome K Jerome's *Three Men in a Boat* (1889). Walk along to the green, turn right into High Street and head to the railway station for your return train.

WHERE TO EAT AND DRINK There is plenty of choice in Windsor, including pubs, restaurants, cafes, bars and tea rooms. Or you might like to try The Royal Stag at Datchet. Overlooking the green and once home to Robert Barker, printer to Elizabeth I, the pub offers snacks and more substantial dishes. There are also cafes and restaurants in Datchet.

WHAT TO SEE As you cross Eton Bridge, which dates from 1823, you can admire not only the views of the river, but the decorative bollards and brass paving set into the bridge by artist Wendy Ramshaw. Note in particular the 'tower bollard', with a lens for viewing the High Street and the castle.

WHILE YOU'RE THERE Guided tours of Eton College run twice most afternoons from late March to late October. The tour lasts around one hour and includes the College Chapel and the Museum of Eton Life. Tours can be booked either by phone or in the visitor centre (opposite the chapel), or purchased on the day before the last tour at 3.15pm.

Sunningdale, Wentworth and Fort Belvedere

DISTANCE 4 miles (6.4km)   MINIMUM TIME 1hr 45min

ASCENT/GRADIENT Negligible ▲ ▲ ▲   LEVEL OF DIFFICULTY ✦ ✦ ✦

PATHS Enclosed woodland paths, estate drive, paths and tracks, path across golf course and polo ground

LANDSCAPE Semi-residential area

SUGGESTED MAP OS Explorer 160 Windsor, Weybridge & Bracknell

START/FINISH Grid reference: SU953676

DOG FRIENDLINESS Lead required across golf course and polo ground

PARKING On-street parking in Sunningdale village

PUBLIC TOILETS None on route

In the closing weeks of 1936 newspaper headlines were dominated by one of the saddest and most dramatic chapters in the history of the monarchy – the abdication of Edward VIII, the uncrowned king who chose to give up the throne for the love of a woman, American divorcee Wallis Simpson. He knew his decision would provoke the strongest disapproval – that what he wanted to do would be at odds with courtly tradition and principles. But Edward stuck to his guns. He was in love with Wallis Simpson, who was not allowed to become Queen because she had been divorced, and he had no intention of giving her up.

FORT BELVEDERE

During the crisis, played out against the backdrops of the House of Commons and the House of Windsor, Edward spent much of his time at Fort Belvedere, his beloved country residence near fashionable Sunningdale. Originally constructed by William, Duke of Cumberland, as a triangular belvedere tower in the 1730s, the building was later enlarged to become a miniature fortress for royal tea parties, the home of a royal collection of guns and for storing various family treasures. A battery of cannon was even installed, to be fired on royal birthdays by a resident bombardier. 'It was a child's idea of a fort', wrote Diana Cooper, a leading figure in royal circles and high society, 'the sentries, one thought, must be of tin'.

It was back in the 1920s, years before the crisis, that the then Prince of Wales asked his father if he could use Fort Belvedere. Something of a playboy, Edward was a noted socialite who liked to entertain regularly and on a lavish scale. He was allowed to take up residence here, but in later years the house became much more than just a country retreat. In the closing stages of the drama, Edward asked his brothers to visit him at Fort Belvedere and witness his signature on the abdication document. It was signed at 12.45pm on Thursday 10 December, 1936, in one of the King's private rooms. A few members of his secretarial staff were present and outside, on the Ascot road, a crowd gathered to see him leave the fort for the last time.

Long after he had given up the throne and gone into exile, Fort Belvedere still occupied his thoughts. In his memoirs, Edward wrote fondly of the house that 'laid hold of me in so many ways'.

Today Fort Belvedere is a private residence, home to Canadian billionaire Galen Weston, who among many business interests owns Selfridges. Weston also part-owns neighbouring Coworth Park, with part of the estate owned by the Brunei Government and run as a polo centre. The public centrepiece is Coworth Park Hotel, a luxury country hotel and spa.

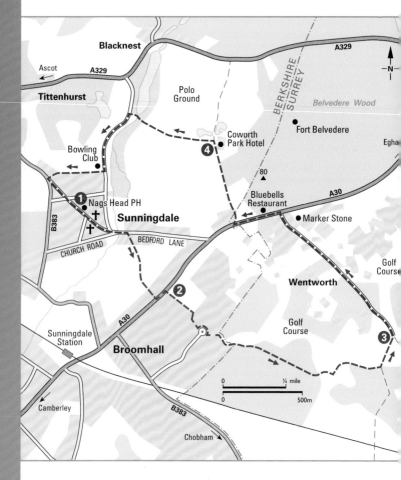

❶ With your back to the Nags Head, turn left and walk down the High Street, keeping the Anglican church on your right and the Baptist church on the left. Pass Church Road and continue along Bedford Lane. Cross a brook and turn right immediately past some bungalows to follow a path cutting between hedgerows and fields. At the A30 turn left, cross the road and walk a short distance to a sign on the right for Shrubs Hill Lane.

2 Follow the leafy path to a junction at a close-board fence and turn right by the bridleway/footpath sign. Curve left, make for a roundabout and swing left, looking for the footpath between 'Rosemullion' and 'Highgate'. Follow it through the woods, round to the right, and when you join a wider path on a bend, keep left. Skirt the golf course, bearing right and keeping the course to your left, cutting between trees and bracken. After passing though a small clump of woodland, veer immediately left and follow the path across the fairways, keeping left at a junction by a bunker. Veer right at the first fork, into the trees, and follow the path – a fairway to your left. The path, becoming tarmac at this point, swings left and across the fairway to a junction with a tarmac drive at a footpath signpost.

3 Turn left and pass through the Wentworth Estate, cutting between exclusive houses with secluded landscaped grounds and imposing entrances. Reaching the A30, turn left and follow the road west. Walk down to the Berkshire/Surrey border and bear sharp right, just before the Bluebells restaurant, to join a right of way (initially gravel), bearing left past South Lodge. Follow the shaded woodland path between beech trees and exposed roots. Beyond the wood you reach the charming, surprisingly rustic-looking buildings of Coworth Park Hotel.

4 When you get to the stone bridge, turn left and follow the waymarked footpath alongside a post and rail fence across a broad expanse of parkland, with polo lawns to right and left. Eventually cross a track on the far side. After a short stretch of woodland, turn left at the road via a gate and pass several houses. When you reach the speed restriction sign, bear right to join a byway by Sunningdale Bowling Club. Keep to a tarmac drive and continue ahead. Turn left at the road, swinging left after 20 paces at the fork. Pass Coworth Road and fork left into the High Street to return to the centre of Sunningdale village.

WHERE TO EAT AND DRINK The Nags Head is conveniently located at the start/finish of the walk. This simple, unspoiled village pub offers snacks and full meals. En route, Bluebells is an excellent restaurant, and you may like to sample the high life by dropping into Coworth Park Hotel, if only for a coffee.

WHAT TO SEE There has never been public access to Fort Belvedere. It may, however, be glimpsed through the trees, depending on the time of year, from Coworth Park Hotel. Call in for a coffee and the staff may be able to help you.

WHILE YOU'RE THERE Keep your eyes peeled for famous faces as you stroll through the Wentworth Estate. Built in the 1920s, its recent residents have included Sarah, Duchess of York, Elton John and Cliff Richard. The Sultan of Brunei, Bruce Forsyth, the golfer Ernie Els and Formula 1 bosses Eddie Jordan and Ron Dennis all currently live here at some time of the year.

Windsor Great Park

DISTANCE 5.25 miles (8.4km)		MINIMUM TIME 2hrs 30min

ASCENT/GRADIENT 160ft (49m) ▲▲▲   LEVEL OF DIFFICULTY ✦✦✦

PATHS Park drives and rides, woodland paths and tracks

LANDSCAPE Sprawling parkland of Windsor Great Park

SUGGESTED MAP OS Explorer 160 Windsor, Weybridge & Bracknell

START/FINISH Grid reference: SU947727

DOG FRIENDLINESS Dogs under strict control or on lead

PARKING Car park by Cranbourne Gate

PUBLIC TOILETS None on route

Walkers in East Berkshire who enjoy peaceful parkland, leafy paths and a sense of space in a noisy and cluttered world don't have to look very far to find what they want. Right on their doorstep is the opportunity to walk for miles and yet remain within the confines of Windsor Great Park, once part of a royal hunting ground and now, in effect, an enormous nature reserve covering thousands of acres, where deer roam amid ancient trees. Windsor Great Park stretches south from Windsor Castle some 5 miles (8km) down to the Surrey border. The northern part is quieter, less commercialised and much less visited than the well-known southern section.

Comprising about 4,800 acres (1,944ha) of wooded parkland and magnificent landscaped gardens, the general design and landscaping of the Great Park is largely the work of George II's son, the Duke of Cumberland, who was given the rangership of Windsor Great Park in recognition of his victory over the Jacobites at the Battle of Culloden in 1746.

One of the park's most striking features is the oak-lined Long Walk, running in a straight line between Windsor and the mighty equestrian statue of George III on Snow Hill. This was erected in 1831 and is familiarly known as the Copper Horse.

COPPER HORSE VIEWS

From the statue of the Copper Horse you can enjoy one of the most famous views in Britain of Windsor Castle. In fact, during your walk the castle will come into view several times. During the late 1950s the exiled Duke of Windsor said of the royal residence and its surroundings: *'there is one place...which hardly changes at all, and that is Windsor Castle. Here is a palace essentially English in character. I take pleasure in the way it broods, with an air of comfortable benevolence, down over the homely town of Windsor, while to the south spreads the spacious Great Park, with the Long Walk stretching three miles through the soft, green English landscape and the meadows of the Home Park to the south, refreshed by the waters of the slowly winding Thames.'*

But it is not just royalty and ramblers who love Windsor Great Park. To the surprise of many visitors there is a lively village here, complete with post office and shop, along with excellent sports facilities. It was built in the 1930s to house royal estate workers. Less surprisingly, many writers have been captivated and inspired by the Park. Alexander Pope often rode here and wrote about the scenery, while Jonathan Swift described the Long Walk as 'the finest avenue I ever saw'.

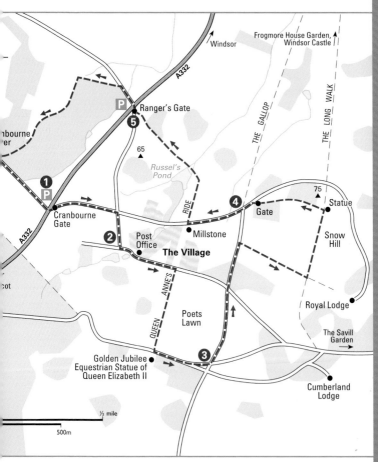

❶ From the car park, cross the A332 to Cranbourne Gate and enter the park. Follow the drive alongside trees planted over the years to commemorate Queen Victoria's Golden Jubilee in 1887 and Edward VII's coronation in 1902. To the left are distant views of Windsor Castle.

Turn right at the first crossroads, signposted 'Cumberland Lodge', and follow the drive to the next junction by two ponds where swans are often seen.

❷ Keep left here, signposted 'The Village'. Pass the Post Office and

General Store, walk between a spacious green and a playing field, and then turn right, off the track, to join the broad, grassy Queen Anne's Ride, heading towards an equestrian statue. Look back for another view of Windsor Castle. Follow the ride to a tarmac drive and the equestrian statue of Queen Elizabeth II, erected for her Golden Jubilee. Turn left, keep left at the fork, then left again after a few paces at a crossroads.

❸ Continue ahead at the next junction and then, 200yds (183m) beyond the woods, turn right to follow a broad, hedge-lined, grassy path. Ahead lies Royal Lodge and to the left of it is the famous Copper Horse statue. Take the next grassy ride on the left and head for a deer gate. Through this, keep ahead towards the statue, cross a bridleway, and when you draw level with the statue bear left. The figure of George III points the way to a woodland path, which merges with a sandy bridleway running down to a drive. Pass through the gate and keep right at the immediate fork.

❹ Walk along to Queen Anne's Ride, which crosses the drive just before a house. On the left is a millstone. Turn right here and follow the ride to Russel's Pond. Veer left and walk beside the pond and fence. Go straight ahead (right) as the path forks left and right. Continue uphill through woodland, then drop down to the road at Ranger's Gate.

❺ Cross over at the lights and take the tarmac drive beyond the car park. Just before white gates leading into Flemish Farm, turn left and follow a sandy bridleway alongside a field. Continue up the slope and through the wood. After 0.5 miles (800m), on a left bend, veer right along a narrow path between trees. When it reaches a gate (marked 'Private Area No Admittance') turn left and keep alongside a fence. The path is completely overgrown in some places, and disappears intermittently amid fallen trees and tall undergrowth. However, as long as you keep following the fence it will reappear. Eventually you reach a drive. On the right is Cranbourne Tower. Turn left to return to the car park.

WHERE TO EAT AND DRINK Light refreshments at the Post Office and General Store in the village is the only option on this route unless you bring a picnic. Established in 1948, the shop is open on weekdays from 7.30am to 4pm, closing at 1pm on Wednesday and Friday. On Saturday it opens 8:30am to 3.30pm, and on Sunday 10am to 3.30pm. It has a pleasant garden area with benches.

WHAT TO SEE On Queen Anne's Ride stands a millstone, unveiled to commemorate the planting of the first of 1,000 trees here, marking 1,000 years of the office of High Sheriff of Windsor Great Park. Near the end of the walk, Cranbourne Tower is part of a lodge once visited by Samuel Pepys in 1665, and where Queen Victoria used to take tea.

WHILE YOU'RE THERE Frogmore House Garden, just off the Long Walk, is the last resting place of Queen Victoria and Prince Albert. The mausoleum, built by Victoria, sits in a splendid landscaped garden with an 18th-century lake. Frogmore is only open to the public on a limited number of days during the year, so check ahead.

Right: The Long Walk entrance to Windsor Castle (Walk 25)

Windsor Great Park and Virginia Water

DISTANCE 7.75 miles (12.5km)	**MINIMUM TIME** 3hrs

ASCENT/GRADIENT Negligible ▲ ▲ ▲   **LEVEL OF DIFFICULTY** ✦ ✦ ✦

PATHS Park drives and rides, woodland paths and tracks

LANDSCAPE Sprawling parkland of Windsor Great Park, lake and ponds

SUGGESTED MAP OS Explorer 160 Windsor, Weybridge & Bracknell

START/FINISH Grid reference: SU976722

DOG FRIENDLINESS Dogs under strict control or on lead

PARKING On the road by Bishopsgate

PUBLIC TOILETS Visitor Pavilion, by main car park on A30

The southern half of Windsor Great Park is by far the most popular part of the park for good reason – visitors come on foot, on horseback and on two wheels to enjoy its famous gardens, peaceful ponds, lakeside trail and various eclectic points of interest which range from Classical ruins to a full-sized 100ft (30m) high totem pole from British Columbia. Summer weekends are best if you want to see the 'sport of kings' played at the famous Guards Polo Club, but beware – this is also when the crowds are at their peak.

AROUND VIRGINIA WATER

Picturesque Virginia Water lake, some 7 miles (11.3 km) in circumference, dates back to 1753 when it evolved quite prosaically as a drainage system for the Great Park. When created it was the largest man-made lake in Britain. The origin of its name is unclear, though it may be named for Elizabeth I, the Virgin Queen. There are two curiosities on its southern shore. The Cascade, or waterfall, is made up of giant rocks said to be the remains of a Saxon settlement brought from nearby Bagshot Heath. Probably even older are the stones near by, from the Roman city of Leptis Magna (in present-day Libya).

In the 17th century more than 600 columns from here had been presented to Louis XIV for use in his palaces at Versailles and Paris. In 1816 Britain's Consul-General in Tripoli persuaded the local Governor that the Prince Regent would also like some of the ruins, and permission was given to remove columns and stones. This outraged the local populace, more from a practical viewpoint than a sense of heritage, as they found the stones useful themselves for building and as mill stones. They sabotaged the British efforts, and many statues and columns were destroyed as they were waiting to be loaded onto the ship – in fact three large columns, intended for shipping, still lie on the beach today.

After a spell in the British Museum the Roman remains arrived in the park in 1827, reduced by now to little more than a mish-mash of assorted columns and stones. They were rearranged into a ruined temple folly, as part of the picturesque landscaping at Virginia Water, reflecting the fashion of the late Georgian period. The Cascade and Five-Arch Bridge are also remnants of the park's ornamental heyday.

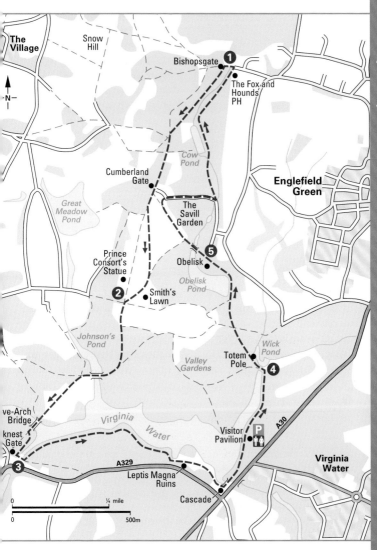

1 Entering the park via Bishopsgate, go straight on for around 50yds (46m), then take the footpath running off diagonally left beside the gravel and sand bridleway. Cross two small footbridges and bear left across a (dry) stream. Cross the bridleway, following the path to the right, then veer right and continue ahead to join the paved road at a plaque commemorating the coronation of King George VI. Follow the road straight on, go past the houses and through Cumberland Gate. You can walk straight across grassy Smith's Lawn if no polo is in progress; otherwise keep right on the main road. Pass the equestrian Prince Consort's Statue (dedicated to Albert) on your right, and leave the polo grounds via the southwest corner, by the main road.

2 Continue downhill, crossing the bridge with Johnson's Pond, right, and Virginia Water lake, left. Immediately after the bridge veer left to a footpath and go straight ahead, past houses to your left. Rejoin the road at the Five-Arch Bridge (built between 1822 and 1827). Cross the bridge, then immediately take the footpath to the left, following the lakeside, with Blacknest Gate to your right.

3 Continue along the southern shore of the lake, eventually reaching the ruins of Leptis Magna (on the right) and opposite, on the lakeside, the old Pond Head. Continue to follow the edge of the lake, passing the Cascade before heading north to the Visitor Pavilion by the main car park on the A30. Keep ahead by the lake.

4 Leaving the lake behind, cross the water again at Wick Pond (look out

for unusual ornamental waterfowl such as Mandarin ducks and Egyptian geese) and go on to the Totem Pole, erected in 1858 to mark the centenary of British Columbia. (In spring you may wish to detour left at this point to explore Valley Gardens). Continue straight ahead, veering slightly right to pick up the main paved path. At the next crossroads continue ahead following the sign towards The Saville Garden. Pass the Obelisk Pond to your left, then the Obelisk itself, dedicated to William, Duke of Cumberland.

5 Take the red gravel path straight on and over a humpback bridge to cross the northern extremity of the pond. Join a broad, grassy path with the polo grounds to the left. As Cumberland Gate draws close, turn right, following the end of the railings on your right-hand side to join the road. Continue on past The Savill Garden, to your right, and by a clump of giant rhubarb turn left to join the Rhododendron Ride path. This soon passes Cow Pond. Complete with gazebo and Georgian Bridge, this is particularly attractive in summer when covered in water lilies. Continue straight ahead to rejoin the main road, which leads back on the right to Bishopsgate.

WHERE TO EAT AND DRINK The Fox and Hounds serves upmarket food, with local ales from the Windsor and Eton Brewery, attractive outdoor seating and afternoon tea in summer. Leith's is a treat for visitors to The Savill Garden. There are seasonal refreshment kiosks beside Blacknest Gate, the Obelisk and the Visitor Pavilion.

WHAT TO SEE In addition to all the man-made features, there's a whole host of plants, shrubs and flowers in this southern sector of the park, both wild and cultivated. Pick up information to help you make the most of exploring the park from the Visitor Pavilion.

WHILE YOU'RE THERE The Savill Garden (admission charge) comprises 35 acres (14ha) of interconnecting gardens and exotic woodland and claims to be Britain's finest ornamental garden. The Valley Gardens, open freely all year round, and are particularly beautiful in spring when the rhododendrons, azaleas, camellias and magnolias are in bloom.

Littlewick Green and Maidenhead Thicket

DISTANCE 3.5 miles (5.7km)	MINIMUM TIME 1hr 30min

ASCENT/GRADIENT 82ft (25m) ▲▲▲   LEVEL OF DIFFICULTY ✦✦✦

PATHS Field and woodland paths, some road walking

LANDSCAPE Mixture of farmland and woodland to west of Maidenhead

SUGGESTED MAP AA Walker's Map 24 The Chilterns

START/FINISH Grid reference: SU838800

DOG FRIENDLINESS Lead required across farmland, and strict control in woodland

PARKING By green in village of Littlewick Green (but note 'no parking' signs in some parts)

PUBLIC TOILETS None on route

Maidenhead Thicket is one of those places that you might frequently pass by in the car without even realising it's there. From the road only a curtain of trees is visible, but step into Maidenhead Thicket and at once you are in a tranquil world of dense woodland and sunny glades. Lime trees, oaks and horse chestnuts bring colour and life to the well-used paths and tracks, and for a few short weeks every year the ground is covered with violets and hazy blue carpets of bluebells.

HAUNT OF HIGHWAYMEN

Maidenhead Thicket consists of 368 acres (149ha) of woodland and glades. These days it is National Trust land, but it used to be known as a notorious haunt of highwaymen. The trees and bushes lining the Great West Road would have given these 18th-century robbers perfect cover as they lay in wait for passing stage coaches.

Nearby Maidenhead once boasted scores of inns which prospered on the vulnerability of coach passengers. Most opted to stay in the town overnight rather than risk driving through the dreaded thicket at dusk. It is also said that the highwaymen who lurked under the trees preferred the coaches entering the town from the west – those approaching from the east had probably been robbed already by the highwaymen of Hounslow Heath.

DANGEROUS TIMES

Claude Duval (1643–70), one of the most notorious highwaymen, preyed upon travellers in this area. According to a handbook on Berkshire, Buckinghamshire and Oxfordshire, published in 1860, 'in the reign of Elizabeth, the vicar of Hurley, who served the cure of Maidenhead, was allowed an extra salary to atone for the danger of passing the thicket'. The most famous highwayman of all, Dick Turpin (1705–39), travelled this way too, waiting in the shadows to ambush any passing coaches. From here he galloped to his aunt's cottage at nearby Sonning where he stabled his trusty horse Black Bess before going into hiding in Oxfordshire, waiting until the dust settled.

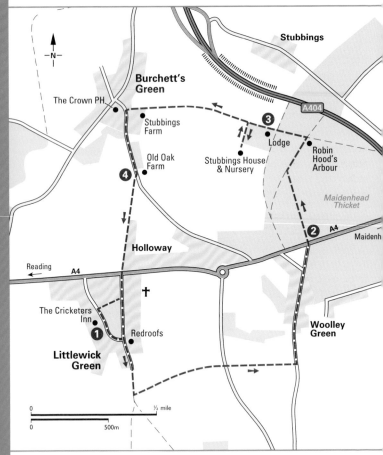

1 Head for the southeast corner of the green (furthest away from the A4) in the centre of Littlewick Green. Pass Redroofs Theatre School, continue into School Lane and follow it past a 'Motor Vehicles Prohibited' sign to the woodland edge. Emerging from the trees, bear left to join a tarmac track running across the fields, with a hedge on your left. There are good views south along here. Cross a

road leading to a business park and continue over farmland to the next road. Turn left, passing houses, and cross the A4 (beware traffic).

2 You are now entering Maidenhead Thicket. Follow the waymarked path between trees and clearings, soon merging with a path from the left. After some tall oaks you will reach a (muddy) bridleway: veer right and follow the main route (there may be tyre tracks), bearing left at the butterfly waymarker. The next crossroads of footpath is known as Robin Hood's Arbour. Turn left and follow the hard path to Stubbings House lodge on your left.

❸ Cross to the kissing gate, right of the lodge. Make a short diversion here to Stubbings House itself, following the cafe sign pointing left. Retrace your steps then follow the path out, left, across the fields through two kissing gates. The footpath, initially with a hedge on the left, becomes a track before reaching Stubbings Farm buildings. At the road at Burchett's Green, turn left and pass Little Stubbings with its white weatherboarded dovecote tower, Old Manor Cottage, and Stubbings Manor, with ornate brickwork and a delightful garden. Follow the lane and veer right, opposite the entrance to Old Oak Farm, onto Knowl Hill Bridleway Circuit.

❹ Follow the path between hedgerows and trees. Further on it runs beside houses and bungalows. Along this stretch the path broadens to a track, and the sound of traffic on the A4 gradually becomes audible. At the junction go straight over the A4 into Jubilee Road and follow it back towards the cricket ground at Littlewick Green. Note the entrance to the village churchyard, somewhat hidden, to your left-hand side just off the green. On reaching the edge of the green, bear right to join a waymarked footpath running alongside the ground and past the front of Littlewick Green cricket club. Note the thatched cottage in the centre of the green, partly protected by trees but still perilously close to the southern boundary of the cricket pitch. Beside it is a pretty row of cottages. At the road turn left, passing The Cricketers Inn. Alternatively, follow the road round the eastern edge of the green to return to your car.

WHERE TO EAT AND DRINK Standing in the shadow of a walnut tree, The Cricketers at Littlewick Green is a charming pub overlooking the village's lovely cricket ground. The Crown at Burchett's Green is a well-established village local, with an assortment of food. The cafe at Stubbing's Nursery is set in a lovely glasshouse, and its terrace looks onto an 18th-century walled garden full of shrubs and plants for sale.

WHAT TO SEE In the corner of Littlewick Green lies a house called Redroofs, now a theatre school. This was once the home of Ivor Novello (1893–1951), the Welsh matinee idol and contemporary of Noël Coward, who became one of Britain's most prolific playwrights and composers. It was at Redroofs that Novello composed several of his most famous musicals. Stubbings House was the home of Queen Wilhelmina of Holland during World War II, when her own residence was occupied by the Nazis. Her bodyguard camped at Robin Hood's Arbour.

WHILE YOU'RE THERE Stop for a few moments at Robin Hood's Arbour, in the heart of Maidenhead Thicket, and imagine this place as an Iron Age enclosure, probably dating back to just before the Roman conquest. The origin of the name probably stems from the fact that outlaws in general at this time were known as 'Robin Hoods', and of course Maidenhead Thicket was notorious for its highwaymen.

Around Burchett's Green

DISTANCE 4 miles (6.4km)   MINIMUM TIME 1hr 45min

ASCENT/GRADIENT 262ft (80m) ▲▲▲   LEVEL OF DIFFICULTY +++

PATHS Field and woodland paths

LANDSCAPE Mixture of farmland and woodland to west of Maidenhead

SUGGESTED MAP AA Walker's Map 24 The Chilterns

START/FINISH Grid reference: SU841813

DOG FRIENDLINESS Lead required across farmland and on college property

PARKING There is no on-street parking on this route, but pub patrons may use the car parks at The Crown, or at the Dewdrop Inn near Point ❺ (both are closed on Mondays)

PUBLIC TOILETS None on route

The history of grand red-brick Hall Place dates back nearly 800 years, to the time when La Halle, the manor house of Hurley (immediately north of here) was built. Throughout the centuries the estate underwent many changes of hands, and the current Georgian pile was built between 1728 and 1735 by William East, a London lawyer who held the lease of the Manor of Kennington. Hall Place remained in the Clayton East family for over 200 years. The final heir, Richard, died in the 1930s. He was a Royal Navy pilot, and he and his young wife Dorothy, also a qualified pilot, were the inspiration for the tragic young English aristocratic couple in Michael Ondaatje's 1992 novel *The English Patient*, which went on to become a hugely successful movie.

ANIMAL FARM

In 1948 Hall Place was sold to the Ministry of Agriculture and then acquired by Berkshire County Council. Today the ground floor of the house is a conference and functions venue (popular in summer for weddings), and around it sprawls the campus of Berkshire College of Agriculture (BCA). Its higher education courses include equestrian, animal care and veterinary studies, and its extensive estate is a fascinating place. As you walk through it you will see aviaries (including exotic breeds), kennels and dog-training facilities, science laboratories, and fields and paddocks stocked with cattle, goats and rare breeds of sheep and pigs, plus exotic species such as wallabies, rheas and llamas, and rare British wildlife such as Scottish wildcats and red squirrels. The estate is managed for both arable and livestock farming to support the college curriculum.

The landscaped grounds and gardens to the west of the house have an uninterrupted view of fields and woods beyond, and its verdant lawns are bordered by mature trees, several of which were planted in Victorian times. These are lovingly maintained by the college to provide both a natural framework for the grand mansion, and for the enjoyment and interest of students and visitors. The back lawn of the house (enquire at reception to see if access is possible) contains a cock-fighting pit, in the form of an amphitheatre, and an elaborate 10-sided candy-pink beehouse. This was built in 1870 and is the finest surviving example of its kind.

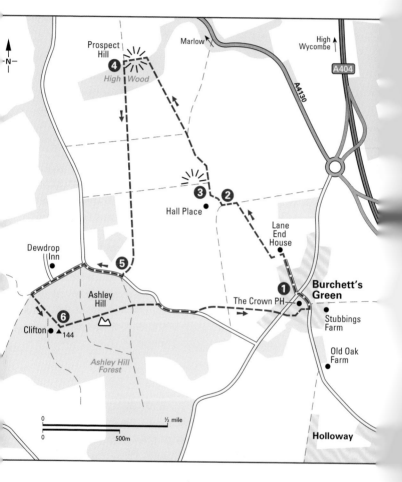

1 Cross the road opposite The Crown pub, diagonally left into Hall Place Lane, and keep left at the entrance to Lane End House. Continue to a gate and then walk straight ahead, following a grassy path across the field to an avenue of lime trees. Turn left and head along the drive towards Hall Place.

2 Swing right in front of Hall Place and go past various buildings and car parks. After the General Teaching Building, veer left at the waymarker, with bird aviaries to the right. Continue past more enclosures; to the left are views over fields and paddocks. Emerge from the enclosures to a startling 180-degree vista. To the right and left broad pathways head off across fields, while straight ahead a broad grassy path, divided by an island of trees, plunges down into a dip then ascends to woodland.

❸ Continue ahead, to the right-hand side of the trees. To the right of a galvanized gate, take the kissing gate to enter High Wood. Go straight ahead to a wire fence which provides a spectacular balcony with views north over the Thames Valley. Swing left, following the fence, to reach a kissing gate and waymarker.

❹ Turn left to return through the wood, parallel to the path on which you entered. Leave the wood, heading down the hill. Continue straight ahead through another kissing gate, between the fields of the BCA, towards the tree-clad slopes of Ashley Hill. Continue straight on, into the last field, via a short ascent of steps, and continue along its left-hand edge, passing wooden showjumping ditches. Pass a house and go through a kissing gate to the road.

❺ Turn right and follow the woodland edge. Go straight ahead at the bend, passing the turning to the Dewdrop Inn, hidden away in a hollow in the woods. Continue ahead to the left of a 'private' sign, and follow the path to a waymarked junction. Turn sharp left, making a steep ascent through the trees. Pass over a crossing track and keep left at the fork. Ahead is the entrance to Clifton, an isolated house.

❻ Turn left and follow the steep drive down through the woods. As it eventually sweeps to the right, go straight ahead on a paved path which runs to the road. Turn right, and when the road begins to curve to the right look for a footpath branching left through the trees. Go through a kissing gate and skirt a fence and (hidden) stream. Follow the path over a track by a gate and keep ahead towards houses. Walk beside the houses, through a kissing gate, cross the road and look for two paths opposite. Bear left through the wood for a short distance until you come to Furze Cottage on your left. Emerge onto the road opposite Little Stubbings, turn left and The Crown is just around the corner, a few paces to your left.

WHERE TO EAT AND DRINK Refreshments are restricted to the two pubs on this route, The Crown and the Dewdrop Inn. Both put an emphasis on dining, with most food – including bread – home-made on the premises. The Dewdrop Inn is the more interesting of the two historically, dating back to the 1600s and supposedly used by highwayman Dick Turpin. Both pubs are closed on Monday during the day.

WHAT TO SEE Look out in the fields for the handiwork of the college students, who have carved tree trunks and other pieces of wood into crocodiles, fish and other things. These are used as poles and fences for the showjumping competitions which take place here. You may also notice the remains of a brick pyramid, which once stood on top of an ice house.

WHILE YOU'RE THERE The village of Cookham, with its gallery dedicated to artist Stanley Spencer (see Walk 31), is less than 6 miles (9.7km) northeast of Burchett's Green.

Stanley Spencer's Cookham

DISTANCE 6 miles (9.7km)   MINIMUM TIME 2hrs

ASCENT/GRADIENT Negligible ▲▲▲   LEVEL OF DIFFICULTY ✚✚✚

PATHS Pavements, riverside promenade and Thames Path

LANDSCAPE Riverside, fields and meadows

SUGGESTED MAP AA Walker's Map 24 The Chilterns

START/FINISH Grid reference: SU887807

DOG FRIENDLINESS Lead required through villages and Maidenhead

PARKING Maidenhead Station

PUBLIC TOILETS Maidenhead Station

NOTES This walk from Maidenhead to Cookham returns via the railway – check train times ahead

This lovely walk takes in one of the most beautiful stretches of the whole River Thames. King of the riverside mansions is Cliveden, perched high above the Thames (most visible in winter), on the opposite bank to the walk. This Italianate mansion was once the home of the wealthy and influential Astor family. Boulter's Lock is one of the most famous stopping points on the Thames and was where the cream of society (including prime minsters and noblemen) gathered at many river events before World War I, often before being entertained at Cliveden.

BIRTHPLACE OF AN ARTIST

Cookham is a beautiful little village that will forever be associated with the artist Stanley Spencer (1891–1959). He called Cookham 'a village in Heaven', and was a controversial and eccentric figure. Spencer was born in Cookham High Street and spent most of his life in the village. The former Methodist chapel on the corner of the High Street, to which Mrs Spencer marched young Stanley and her eight other children every Sunday, is now an important gallery devoted to his work.

Cookham played a key role in Spencer's work, forming the setting for many biblical and figure paintings, as well as landscapes. The gallery's most famous painting is *The Last Supper*, painted in 1920, but also notable, and very relevant to this walk are *View from Cookham Bridge* and *Christ Preaching at Cookham Regatta*. You can also see the pram in which he wheeled his paints and brushes around the village when painting landscapes.

Today Spencer's works are highly prized, and in 2011 *Sunflower and Dog Worship* sold at auction for £5.4 million.

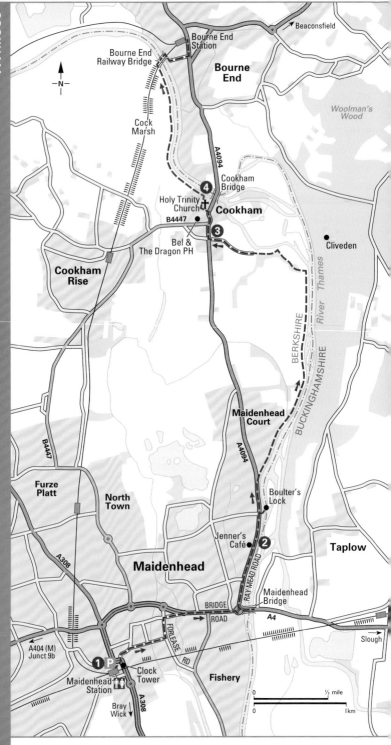

Beaconsfield

Bourne End Station

Bourne End Railway Bridge

Bourne End

Woolman's Wood

Cock Marsh

A4094

4 Cookham Bridge

Holy Trinity Church

Cookham

B4447

3

Bel & The Dragon PH

Cookham Rise

Cliveden

River Thames

BERKSHIRE

BUCKINGHAMSHIRE

Maidenhead Court

A4094

B4447

Furze Platt

North Town

Boulter's Lock

A308

Jenner's Café

2

Taplow

Maidenhead

RAY MEAD ROAD

Maidenhead Bridge

BRIDGE

A4

Slough

ROAD

FORLEASE RD

1 P

Clock Tower

Maidenhead Station

Fishery

Bray Wick

A308

0   ½ mile

0   1km

1 Walk down to the clock tower, cross the road at the lights and bear right into Queen Street, by the Bell pub. Veer right into York Road and pass the football club. Walk down to the mini-roundabout and turn left into Forlease Road. Head for the next junction and turn right into Moorbridge Road. Walk through the underpass and veer right/straight ahead on the far side, following Bridge Road towards Maidenhead Bridge, and passing almshouses on your left. Cross the bridge almost to the opposite bank and look to the right, downstream, to see Brunel's railway bridge, depicted in J M W Turner's *Rain, Steam and Speed* (1844). Return to the Maidenhead side of the river, go through the small gardens and bear right into Ray Mead Road, passing Jenner's Cafe.

2 Continue to Boulter's Lock. You can divert here to cross the bridge and walk around Boulter's Restaurant onto Ray Mill Island. Return to the main road, and where the road and Thames Path divide, follow the tow path. The view to the Buckinghamshire bank is dominated by the woods of the Cliveden Estate. The path swings away from the river and cuts through woodland, eventually merging to join a paved road (Mill Lane). Continue ahead to the junction, turn right and follow the road into Cookham.

3 Pass the Stanley Spencer Gallery, and Cookham High Street is on your left. Take a few minutes to browse its pretty shops and buildings – Bel and The Dragon, built in 1417, is one of the oldest licensed houses in England. Turn left out of the High Street to continue, passing a large boulder known as the Tarry Stone, once the meeting point for the local 'Olympic' games. Continue ahead, and soon turn left at the entrance to Holy Trinity Church. A few yards further on, to the left of the path, is Spencer's modest marble memorial. Continue past the church and veer left to rejoin the Thames Path, looking back right to see Cookham Bridge.

4 Swing left and pass Cookham Reach Sailing Club via two gates. Cross the meadow and walk by the river, eventually passing through a kissing gate into Cock Marsh water meadow. Ahead is Bourne End railway bridge. Go through a kissing gate, pass beneath the bridge and turn immediately left. Go up the steps and cross the footbridge to the Buckinghamshire bank. Once over the bridge, go through a gate, turn right into an alleyway and pass a house called River Haven. Keep left at this point and follow the drive alongside a brick wall to the road. Turn left to the station at Bourne End to catch the train back to Maidenhead.

WHERE TO EAT AND DRINK Both Maidenhead and Cookham offer a wide choice of eating places and pubs – Bel and The Dragon at Cookham has a beautiful garden and is by far the best for food. Jenner's Cafe is set in pretty gardens, while Boulter's Restaurant and Bar overlooks the famous lock at Point **2**.

WHAT TO SEE On Boulter's Lock Island bridge is a blue plaque dedicated to the broadcaster Richard Dimbleby, who once lived here. In front of the restaurant is 'Kiosk No. 1', a curious bright green public telephone box with a pyramid roof. This is a rare survivor of the first standard type of post office telephone kiosk introduced in 1921. It was allowed its striking green colour (as opposed to regulation red), because of its lockside location.

Up Bowsey Hill from Wargrave

DISTANCE 6 miles (9.7km)	MINIMUM TIME 2hrs 15min

ASCENT/GRADIENT 248ft (76m) ▲▲▲   LEVEL OF DIFFICULTY ✦✦✦

PATHS Stretches of road, field and woodland paths; several stiles

LANDSCAPE High ground on upper slopes of Thames Valley, dense woodland and peaceful glades

SUGGESTED MAP AA Walker's Map 24 The Chilterns

START/FINISH Grid reference: SU786785

DOG FRIENDLINESS Lead required around livestock and where requested by signs

PARKING Public car park (pay-and-display) in School Lane, just off A321, right immediately past The Bull

PUBLIC TOILETS None on route

The riverside village of Wargrave is usually quiet during the week, but often busy with visitors and boating enthusiasts at the weekends, particularly in the summer. It is sometimes mistakenly believed that the village has a connection with military cemeteries. That couldn't be further from the truth – its name actually means 'grove by the weirs'.

The village is distinctly Edwardian in appearance, but its origins date back many centuries. When Edith, the wife of Edward the Confessor, held the manor in the 11th century, it was known as Weregrave. The church among the trees dates from World War I, replacing an earlier building that, except for the Norman tower, was destroyed by fire on Whit Sunday, 1914. It is believed that the fire was the work of a militant wing of the Suffragettes – angry because the vicar would not withdraw the word 'obey' from the marriage service. However, this claim was never proved. Madame Tussaud's daughter-in-law Elizabeth is buried in the churchyard.

COLOURFUL RESIDENTS

Wargrave seems to have produced more than its fair share of colourful characters over the centuries. One of them was Zachary Allnutt who lived for more than a hundred years at Lavender Cottage on the Henley road. Allnutt was a well-known local lavender grower in the 19th century.

Another colourful resident was Thomas Day, the 18th-century idealist and author of *Sandford and Merton* (1783), a tale of two boys – one rich, the other poor. Day was an eccentric character but a genial man, nonetheless. He supported the abolition of slavery and the protection of animals from cruelty. He believed, too, that animals responded to kindness and gentleness. However, this proved to be his undoing. One day in 1789, in an attempt to demonstrate his conviction, he mounted an unbroken horse and was subsequently thrown off and killed.

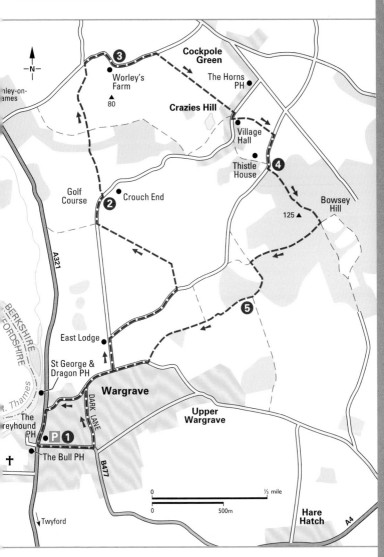

① From the car park turn left and walk along School Lane (the B477). On the first bend bear left into Dark Lane, head up the hill and turn right at the T-junction into Wargrave Hill. Follow the road and turn left at the sign for Crazies Hill. Turn right opposite

East Lodge towards Warren Row, follow the winding lane and turn left through a wooden picket gate to join a waymarked path. Keep alongside the fence, and after 200yds (183m) fork left at the broken footpath sign, across the fields towards trees. Go through a gate and turn right at the road. Continue for 150yds (137m), veering left through a kissing gate.

② Now on a golf course, keep close to the left boundary of the field, go straight ahead, then descend steeply (be careful in wet weather) to a kissing gate (keep to the right-hand side as it is partially hidden) and a bridleway beyond. Cross a stile almost opposite and climb the steep hillside. Over a stile at the crest keep ahead on the higher ground, following the path alongside the fence. Descend to a kissing gate at the road and turn immediately right. Head uphill and pass Worley's Farm.

③ Take the next waymarked path on the right, just before a row of trees, and cross a stile. Walk between fences and hedges, going through a kissing gate near the crest and lining up with a large white house in the distance. Keep to the left of the house, Crazies, whose portico was salvaged from the old Henley Town Hall. Go through a kissing gate and follow an enclosed path to the road. Turn right, then almost immediately left beside the village hall. Follow the path by a paddock to a kissing gate by the road. Turn right and keep going past

the entrance to Thistle House (and a byway, the Chiltern Way, into trees on the right) to a gate on the left.

④ Join a woodland path and look out for white arrows on the tree trunks, eventually reaching a waymarked junction. Turn right here, avoiding a path on the right, and keep going to the next waymarked junction, on the edge of the wood. Fields are visible here. Bear left and walk down to a flight of steps and a footbridge. Go straight on to the edge of the field, to a public footpath sign, and turn right along the field-edge.

⑤ Cross a bridleway via two stiles and continue ahead along the woodland edge. Look for a hedge gap on the right, cross into the adjoining field and maintain the same direction. Make for a kissing gate and a footbridge in the field corner and continue ahead to the remains of a wrought-iron kissing gate. Follow the path across the next field, heading towards trees. Make for a kissing gate leading out to the road and turn right. Follow it down to the A321, looking out for 'Barrymore', a splendid three-storey house on the right. Turn left and walk along to School Lane to return to the car park.

WHERE TO EAT AND DRINK There are several pubs in Wargrave, among them The Bull, The Greyhound and The St George and Dragon with its lovely riverside terrace. If you want to stop midway round the walk, try The Horns at Crazies Hill.

WHAT TO SEE The pretty hamlet of Crazies Hill lies on the upper slopes of the valley. There is a rather charming story behind its name. Apparently buttercups were once commonplace in this area, and 'crazies' is a rustic country name for buttercups. Look out for the entrance to Thistle House. In the 1960s this was the home of David Greig, a butcher who began a supermarket chain. His emblem was the thistle, and the house was used as a training college for a while.

WHILE YOU'RE THERE As you approach Crazies Hill, look across the fields on the left towards nearby Cockpole Green. It is believed there was once a cockpit here, where cock fighting took place.

Dinton Pastures Country Park

DISTANCE 3 miles (4.8km)	MINIMUM TIME 1hr 30min

ASCENT/GRADIENT Negligible ▲▲▲   LEVEL OF DIFFICULTY ✚✚✚

PATHS Lakeside and riverside paths, some road walking

LANDSCAPE Extensive lakeland

SUGGESTED MAP OS Explorer 159 Reading, Wokingham & Pangbourne

START/FINISH Grid reference: SU784718

DOG FRIENDLINESS Dogs under control and on lead where requested

PARKING Large car park at Dinton Pastures

PUBLIC TOILETS Dinton Pastures

Dinton Pastures Country Park describes itself as a mosaic of rivers, meadows, lakes and woodland. The lakes are old gravel workings that were flooded to form the focal point of this attractive recreational area. Paths and self-guided trails enable visitors to explore this tranquil world of water and wildlife at will.

THE EARLY DAYS

The park's river meadows were once farmed by Anglo-Saxons who called the area Whistley – *wisc* meaning 'marshy meadow' and *lei,* a 'wooded glade' or clearing. The River Loddon was used as part of the same process, farmed for its supply of eels, which were caught in willow traps for the monks of Abingdon Abbey. Traps were still in regular use as late as the 1930s.

By the beginning of the 17th century much of the area formed part of Windsor Forest, where the monarch and his courtiers hunted for pleasure. It was the courtiers who built some of the region's grandest houses, including High Chimneys, to be close to Windsor Castle, the royal powerhouse just 15 miles (24km) east. High Chimneys' farmhouse dates back to 1904. During the mid-1920s it was occupied by a farmer who named the farm after his home village of Dinton, near Aylesbury.

Dinton Pastures forms part of the Loddon's flood plain and is a rich source of gravel, which has been extracted here for more than 100 years. There was an extensive extraction programme here during the late 1960s and through the 1970s. Much of the material was used to construct the M4 and the A329(M), connecting Reading and Wokingham.

RECREATIONAL AREA

Comprising about 230 acres (93ha) and opened in 1979, Dinton Pastures attracts lots of visitors who come here to walk, fish, picnic and indulge in birding – it's a welcome green space on Reading's doorstep. The largest of the lakes here is Black Swan. The Emm Brook once flowed where the lake is now situated. It was later diverted, and the oaks which you can see on the island in the lake once stood on the banks of the old stream.

All the lakes draw a variety of wetland birds such as swans, geese, coots and moorhens. The park's rarest birds are bitterns – fewer than 20 pairs breed in Britain annually. In spring migrants, including nightingales, also make the journey from Africa to nest here.

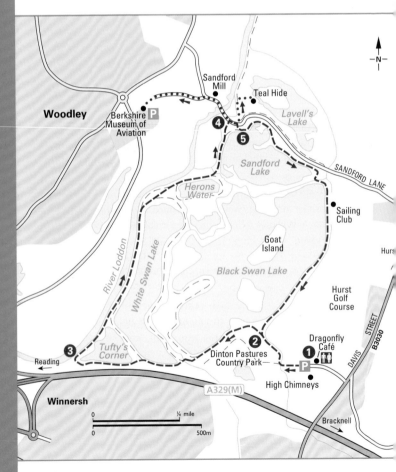

❶ With the Dragonfly Café on the right and High Chimneys behind you, cross the car park to the site map. Follow the wide path and keep right at the fork by the 'wildlife trails' sign.

Pass an enclosed play area on the left, keep the Emm Brook on the right, and enjoy the tantalising glimpses of Black Swan Lake up ahead.

2 Swing left on reaching the water and follow the path beside the lake. When it veers right, turn left across a bridge to a sign for Tufty's Corner. Bear right here and keep left at the fork after a few paces. Follow the path beside White Swan Lake to a waymarker post by a patch of grass and a flight of steps. Avoid the steps, but take the left-hand path and follow it to the lake known as Tufty's Corner. On reaching a junction by a bridge, turn right and keep the River Loddon on your left.

3 Walk along to the next bridge. Don't cross it; instead continue on the riverside path. White Swan Lake lies over to the right, glimpsed at intervals between the trees. Further on, the path curves to the right, in line with the river, before reaching a sign 'Private fishing – members only'. Join a track on the right here and bear left. Pass alongside Herons Water to a sign 'Sandford Lake Conservation Area and Black Swan Lake'. Turn left and keep Sandford Lake on the right. When the path curves right, go out to the road via a kissing gate.

4 To visit the Berkshire Museum of Aviation, bear left and pass Sandford Mill. Take the road signposted 'No Through Road' on the left, pass several cottages and continue ahead when the road dwindles to a path. The museum is on the left. Retrace your steps to Sandford Mill and keep walking ahead to a footpath and kissing gate on the left. Through this, keep left at the first fork, then right at the second and head for the Teal Hide overlooking the wader scrapes. See if you can spot wading birds from here; look out for green sandpipers and redshanks, ducks, swans, kingfishers and the occasional bittern. Return to the road, cross over and return to the lakeside path.

5 Continue with Sandford Lake on your right. On reaching a sign 'Sandford Lake – wildlife area – dogs under control', veer left over a bridge and turn left. Black Swan Sailing Club can be seen on the left. Continue on the broad path and look out across the lake to Goat Island, noted for its population of goats. On reaching the picnic area overlooking Black Swan Lake, turn left and retrace your steps back to the main car park.

WHERE TO EAT AND DRINK The outstanding Dragonfly Café overlooks a beautifully planted and tended garden with several tables. It serves lunches, teas and main meals, and opens late in summer. If you prefer a pub, try the nearby Castle Inn at Hurst, parts of which date back 1,000 years; it, too, has a pleasant garden.

WHAT TO SEE Sandford Mill, built in 1772, was in use until the mid-1950s, and in 1994 it was converted into a private property. A mill was originally recorded on this site in the Domesday Book. With the trees surrounding it and its picturesque white weatherboarded facade, it creates a pretty picture on the edge of the park.

WHILE YOU'RE THERE You would never guess it today but this was once the site of Woodley Airfield, the centre of a thriving aircraft industry. A Handley Page Herald once flown by Prince Philip, and a Royal Navy Fleet Air Arm Fairey Gannet sit outside the Berkshire Museum of Aviation. Inside the modern hangar are various other planes and aero memorabilia. The museum has limited opening times; call ahead to check, tel 0118 934 0712.

Overleaf: Tudor houses on Rose Street, Wokingham (Walk 34)

Linking Wokingham and Crowthorne

DISTANCE 8.5 miles (13.7km)   MINIMUM TIME 2hrs 45min

ASCENT/GRADIENT Negligible ▲▲▲   LEVEL OF DIFFICULTY ✦✦✦

PATHS Streets, forest and field paths, tracks

LANDSCAPE Town streets and well-wooded countryside

SUGGESTED MAP OS Explorer 159 Reading, Wokingham & Pangbourne

START/FINISH Grid reference: SU812685

DOG FRIENDLINESS Under control in woodland, on lead by paddocks and in town

PARKING Public car parks in Rose Street and Denmark Street

PUBLIC TOILETS Rose Street car park; establishments which are part of the Local Loo scheme (library, shops, cafes etc – look for stickers on doors/windows)

A classic market town, above the modern facades and away from the busy traffic, Wokingham is full of hidden corners and picturesque old buildings. Founded in the 13th century by the Norman-French Bishop Roger le Poore, the town was granted a charter by Elizabeth I in 1583. Until the 19th century Wokingham developed at a slow pace, but in recent years it has grown enormously, its rapid expansion influenced by its close proximity to London and the M4.

At the heart of Wokingham, in the Market Place, stands the Town Hall, dating back to 1860. It was designed in flamboyant Gothic Revival style and now houses shops, cafes and a tourist information office. Just a stone's throw from this is Rose Street, one of Wokingham's hidden treasures and the finest surviving example in Berkshire of a medieval 'enclosed' street. Founded in the early 13th century, Rose Street is wide at one end and narrow at the other. At the far end stands All Saints Church, originally a small Saxon chapel that was enlarged in the 12th century. Number 31 Rose Street was once home to James 'Sooty' Seaward. He was the inspiration for Tom the chimney sweep, the central character in *The Water Babies*, by Charles Kingsley (1863).

At the far end of Broad Street and dating from the mid-16th century is the landmark black-and-white Tudor House, one of Wokingham's most attractive buildings. Until the end of World War I it housed a school, and is now offices.

Just outside the town is one of Britain's most famous public schools. Wellington College was founded as a memorial to the Duke of Wellington, following his victory at Waterloo in 1815. When it first opened, it was a school for the orphans of army officers.

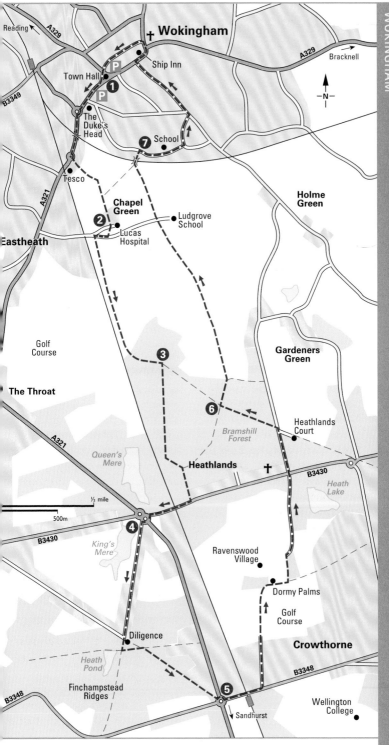

1 With the Town Hall behind you, walk down Denmark Street. Keep right at The Duke's Head. Walk to the roundabout, cross Kendrick Close and Norton Road, and follow Finchampstead Road. Pass under the railway bridge, and take the footpath on the left at the next roundabout, just before Tesco. Pass through a gate, veer right by stables and follow a fenced track between paddocks. Make for a line of houses and continue to the Henry Lucas Hospital Almshouses.

2 Continue ahead on the footpath, then turn right onto a tarmac drive. Pass white gateposts and turn left at a pair of galvanised gates. A long straight stretch of track lies ahead, with the railway to the right. Eventually pass an old wartime Nissen hut and a cottage on the right. About 80yds (73m) further on, turn right by a yellow waymarker post.

3 Follow the track ahead between plantations of trees. After 0.5 miles (800m) reach a T-junction with a small copse ahead; bear right, following waymarkers. Pass a gate and turn right onto the B3430. Continue over the railway bridge, cross Lower Wokingham Road at the roundabout and turn into Hollybush Ride.

4 Continue past several houses. The road finishes, but continue ahead at a junction of tracks into Simon's Wood. Turn left at the next junction. Bear right to follow the byway, keeping right at the gates to 'Heritage'. Follow the track to a roundabout and take the Crowthorne exit. On the right are playing fields of Wellington College.

5 Walk past the station and shops, and turn left into Ravenswood Avenue. Walk along to the Golf Club and follow the drive across the fairways. Look for a footpath sign, and continue with the course now on your right. Pass 'Dormy Palms' and take the next footpath left along the woodland edge. Join a tarmac drive and pass beside the buildings of Ravenswood Village, a community for children with learning difficulties. At traffic lights continue ahead into Heathlands Road. On the left-hand side (opposite the entrance to Heathlands Court), turn left onto a path into Bramshill Forest.

6 Continue ahead and turn right at the next waymarked junction (galvanised gate left), following the 'Health Walk' route. Where the path bends right, go through a deer gate and carry on along the path through the middle of a market garden area. Exit eventually through another gate and continue between fences and fields. Just after a gate marked 'School Grounds' take the narrow path which dives off to the left. Cut between laurel bushes and holly trees, through a dark cover of trees, to go through a gate, cross a drive, and continue ahead. Eventually you will come to a railway footbridge. Cross over it, and when you reach the road (Gypsy Lane) turn right.

7 Follow Gypsy Lane past the school to the next main junction. Cross Murdoch Road and follow Easthampstead Road towards the town centre. Bear right at the T-junction, facing the town's busy one-way system, and walk to the Ship Inn. (Note that the pavement is narrow in front of the Ship Inn as it goes round to the left; if the traffic is busy you may prefer to go around the back of the pub instead.) Follow Wiltshire Road (or Cross Street if you diverted behind the Ship) into Rose Street which leads back, across Broad Street, to the Market Place.

Around California Country Park

DISTANCE 2.75 miles (4.4km)	MINIMUM TIME 1hr 20min

ASCENT/GRADIENT Negligible ▲▲▲ LEVEL OF DIFFICULTY +++

PATHS Well-defined lakeside path and heathland track; unmarked woodland paths and tracks (can be very muddy)

LANDSCAPE Bogland, lowland heath, woods and lake

SUGGESTED MAP OS Explorer 159 Reading, Wokingham & Pangbourne

START/FINISH Grid reference: SU785651

DOG FRIENDLINESS Lead required around livestock and where requested by signs

PARKING Pay-and-display in permitted areas of Country Park

PUBLIC TOILETS At entrance to cafe (no purchase required)

As with much of this area, from around 1300 the present-day village of California formed part of the royal hunting grounds of Windsor Great Forest and remained so until 1901, when Queen Victoria finally disbanded the Royal Buckhounds of Windsor.

FROM BRICKWORKS TO HOLIDAY CAMP

In 1873 John Walter III, grandson of John Walter (founder of *The Times*), began a brick-making industry in the area with excavations on the site of the current country park. The clay that was dug out of here produced some 4.5 million bricks which went into building nearby Bearwood, one of the largest Victorian country houses in England. Formerly Walter's residence, it is now the main building of the prestigious Bearwood public school. Later, bricks from California also went to build *The Times* office at Printing House Square in London. When the brickworks closed the clay pits were flooded to form the present lake.

The family sold the land after World War I, and during the 1920s an entrepreneur named Mr Cartlidge bought up part of California with leisure in mind. He began by operating mystery coach tours from London to here, and these proved so popular that he built a holiday camp, preceding Butlin's and Pontin's by some 10 and 20 years respectively.

California in England, as it was known, reached its zenith in the 1930s with huge numbers coming from London and further afield. The main attraction was its ballroom with a glass floor that lit up in different colours, reputedly recycled from the famous Crystal Palace of 1851. A mini-railway, boating and all kinds of sporting facilities were also on offer. Swimming competitions were held on the lake and there was even an Olympic-size diving board. The site also gained fame for its speedway motorcycle track, which between 1930 and 1950 staged national competitions.

THE POST-WAR YEARS

After World War II chalets were built to accommodate up to 300 guests, and the complex continued to prosper. However, as the 1950s went on, competition increased (from Butlin's, Pontins and others) and the park gradually declined. The grand ballroom became a nightclub in the 1960s but burned down in 1976, never to be rebuilt. During the 1970s the district council began to acquire the land and turned it into what it is today – a multi-recreational area, though on a much reduced scale than in Cartlidge's day. There are still camping facilities, a paddling pool for toddlers, a play area and a heathland of Special Scientific Interest (SSSI).

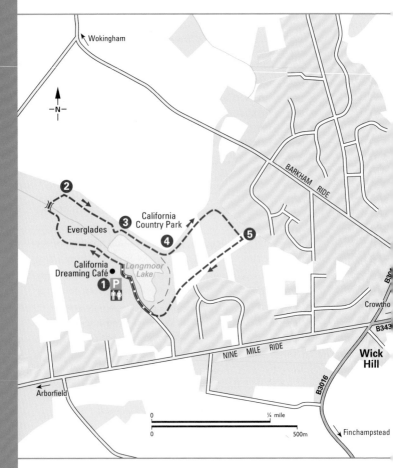

1 With your back to the cafe, walk ahead to the lake and turn left, following the edge clockwise. After a few paces follow it round the bend, then branch off left, signposted 'Everglades'. Continue ahead, through tall trees and through a weighted gate marked 'stock grazing'. You are now entering the heathland SSSI area and the landscape is indeed evocative of Florida's Everglades, albeit on a very small scale and with grass snakes instead of alligators. Cross a small footbridge and continue on the winding path. The next gate takes you onto a long boardwalk. The swampy water to either side is usually completely still, and its bright orange colour is caused by a rare but harmless bacteria.

2 Leave the boardwalk and enter the area known as the Speedway Heath, part of which was used between the 1930s and the 1950s for motorcycle racing. Continue ahead to a fork that diverts briefly off the main path, to a small pond. Shortly after this, look for a small path, no larger than a gap in the trees, to your left. Take a brief diversion from the main path to see the concrete apron (marked out with paint lines) where the motorbike races used to start. Return to the path and ahead is a gate.

3 After a few more paces turn left to rejoin the path heading clockwise around the lake. The lake is no longer used for swimming (on health grounds) but attracts a good number of birds and is popular with anglers who come here for the carp.

4 Take the first path on your left, bearing into the woods. Continue until you see the red roof of a house in front (just outside the woodland perimeter) and take the next turn right onto a narrow path. Continue ahead, keeping the houses to your left.

5 When you come out of the trees you will see a paved path ahead. Turn right on it and follow it back down towards the chalets and touring park area. Bear left, passing though a gap between two posts, and follow the winding path. Turn left across a small boardwalk bridge – over the same type of orange 'swamp water' that you saw in the Everglades earlier – then turn right and continue straight ahead. The lake is now visible to your right. Take the footpath between two posts and follow the path back to the cafe.

WHERE TO EAT AND DRINK The California Dreaming Café serves cooked breakfasts, sandwiches and burgers. There are also picnic tables around the play area. If you want something more substantial, try the Queen's Oak or Tally Ho Eating House in Finchampstead.

WHAT TO SEE Growing out of the rust-coloured waters you will see bright green horsetail – it's a plant that's been around for some 300 million years. Its ancestors were considerably larger, around 20ft (6m) tall, as were the giant dragonflies that would have flown around them, with a wingspan measuring up to 30 inches (76cm).

WHILE YOU'RE THERE Families can head for The Look Out Discovery Centre (6 miles/9.7km east on Nine Mile Ride), a science exhibition which has over 90 hands-on activities for children. Older children (and adventurous adults) can try Go Ape, an aerial ropeway course, also based here.

A circuit at Finchampstead

DISTANCE 5 miles (8km)	MINIMUM TIME 1hr 45min
ASCENT/GRADIENT Negligible ▲▲▲	LEVEL OF DIFFICULTY ✦✦✦

PATHS Mainly field paths and tracks; several stiles

LANDSCAPE Classic farmland on northern side of Blackwater Valley

SUGGESTED MAP OS Explorer 159 Reading, Wokingham & Pangbourne

START/FINISH Grid reference: SU793638

DOG FRIENDLINESS Lead required around livestock

PARKING In vicinity of Finchampstead Church and The Queens Oak

PUBLIC TOILETS None on route

Part of this walk is along an ancient road used by Henry VII and his sons, Arthur and Henry, while hunting in this area. The King had hunting lodges near by at Dogmersfield and Easthampstead Park.

Henry VII had always sought a marriage alliance with Spain for his sons. Katherine of Aragon, the youngest daughter of Ferdinand and Isabella of Spain, and just nine months older than Henry's older son, Prince Arthur, seemed the perfect match. In September 1501 Catherine arrived at Plymouth, and a messenger began the lengthy journey to the King's hunting lodge at Easthampstead to inform His Majesty that the future queen was on her way. A sign on the walk recalls the spot where they heard the news on 16 November.

The King and the princes made their way to the lodge at Dogmersfield, only to find that Katherine had retired for the night and would see no one. Henry was understandably nervous as he had never seen an accurate likeness of Katherine, and insisted on seeing her now. He was apparently relieved to discover she was a pretty girl, with red-gold hair, blue eyes and a fair complexion – a perfect bride for Arthur.

MARRIAGE AND REMARRIAGE

Some 10 days later, the two 15-year-olds were married in St Paul's Cathedral. Tragically, Arthur died six months after the wedding. His untimely death triggered a series of events that would have a momentous effect on the history of England. The King duly passed Katherine on to his younger son, Henry, who married his brother's widow in 1509. As the Church forbade such a union, a special dispensation was obtained from the Pope. Happiness did not follow, however. By 1527, Henry, now King, was desperate for an heir and Katherine had produced no surviving sons. Their only child was a daughter (the future Mary I), but at this time there was no established precedent for a woman on the throne. Having already met and fallen in love with Anne Boleyn, Henry VIII was anxious to dissolve his unfruitful marriage as soon as possible. The Pope refused to bow to his wishes, Henry subsequently broke with the Roman Catholic Church and so began the Reformation in England.

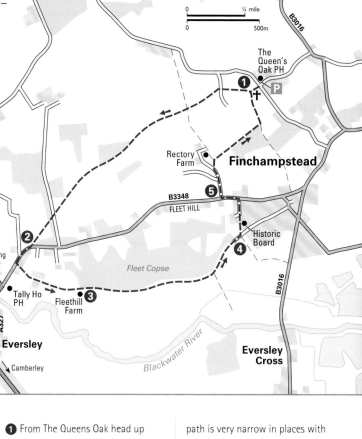

From The Queens Oak head up towards the church. With the church in front, take the lane which forks right and go past White Horse House. The path soon dwindles to a stony track and descends through a wooded tunnel. Cross a lane via two kissing gates and follow a narrow path between tall hedges. Ahead is a waymarked junction. The path follows round to the left, but instead go straight ahead and follow this for several hundred yards. The

path is very narrow in places with tall hedgerows. The hedge drops away in places on the right-hand side, giving good views across fields and beyond. Eventually you will come to a stile. Cross this to reach the B3348 at Fleet Hill.

❷ Turn right and keep on this same side of the main road until you see Vann House opposite. Cross over and, in front of Vann House, follow Fleet Lane (signed 'Public Footpath'). This leads past several houses and ends at Fleethill Farm, where the way appears to be barred by a metal gate. Take the stile to the left of the gate and continue across the farmyard, keeping to the left beside the fenced off woodland – this is a public right of way. Reach another large gate and stile.

❸ Leave the farmyard and continue ahead along a broad path, with paddocks to your right and the woods of Fleet Copse to your left. The paddocks finish, and after passing to the left of another metal gate there is a pair of stiles (one of which is redundant). The path here is much narrower and passes through a field, which is obscured to the right-hand side by a large bund (that is, excavated materials) running along its edge. Continue on until eventually Fleet Copse peters out, the gravel footpath gives way to tarmac and a small housing estate comes into view.

❹ The route turns left, before the houses, onto a footpath – but coming from this direction, both path and waymarker may be obscured by foliage. A few paces further on is a small wooden waymarked sign and a 'historic board', set on a neatly trimmed piece of grass, that records the meeting between the English royals and the Spanish envoy. Retrace your steps a few paces and turn right by the waymarked post. Pass alongside a fence and beneath the boughs of holly trees before emerging onto the B3348, Fleet Hill, with a petrol station immediately to your right.

❺ Turn left and cross the road, then turn right on Rectory Farm Drive. Go past Finchampstead House and Rectory Farm, take the path to the right of the main gate, bear right after about 60yds (55m) and cut between paddocks. Cross the next stile, followed by a footbridge, and turn left, then right. Swing left at the next junction and head for Finchampstead Church. Cut through the churchyard and return to The Queens Oak.

WHERE TO EAT AND DRINK The Queens Oak at the start/end of the walk is a decent pub offering meals and sandwiches, and has a pleasant garden. En route, continue past Vann House (Point ❷), and after another 150yds (137m) is the Tally Ho Eating House, a pub which is part of the Blubeckers chain, known for its ribs, steaks and burgers.

WHAT TO SEE Close to The Queens Oak look out for a plaque encased by creeper which reads: 'The oak tree near this stone was planted 21 June 1887 in commemoration of Queen Victoria's completion of the 50th year of her reign'. The stone was placed here in June 1897 to mark Victoria's Diamond Jubilee.

WHILE YOU'RE THERE Step into Finchampstead Church, built on an ancient earthwork with a steep scarp on three sides. Over the chancel arch are fragments of 12th- and 15th-century wall-paintings.

By the Thames in Reading

DISTANCE 3 miles (4.8km)	MINIMUM TIME 1hr 15min

ASCENT/GRADIENT Negligible ▲▲▲   LEVEL OF DIFFICULTY ✚✚✚

PATHS Pavements, river and canal tow path

LANDSCAPE Urban

SUGGESTED MAP OS Explorer 159 Reading, Wokingham & Pangbourne

START/FINISH Grid reference: SU716735

DOG FRIENDLINESS Lead required in town, under strict control on riverbank

PARKING The Forbury, Chatham Street, Garrard Street, Hexagon

PUBLIC TOILETS Reading Station

Reading's skyline has changed dramatically over the years – riverside office developments have taken the place of many of the older buildings, and the vast Oracle shopping complex is now the glittering jewel in the town centre's crown. However, some of old Reading's landmarks remain – and one of them is the town's gaol where Oscar Wilde languished for 18 months, between November 1895 and May 1897.

THE IMPORTANCE OF BEING OSCAR

It was the 8th Marquess of Queensberry, frustrated by thwarted attempts to break up the scandalous relationship between his son, Lord Alfred Douglas, and Oscar Wilde, who was responsible for the writer's downward spiral. He had publicly insulted Wilde at his home, at his clubs and throughout London's theatreland where many of Wilde's plays were staged.

Caught in the crossfire between father and son, Wilde brought a prosecution for libel against Queensberry, but he lost the case. Queensberry and his cohorts now began plotting to destroy Wilde. They gave evidence against him, testifying to his dubious sexuality and improper practices. The 1885 Criminal Law Amendment Act made sexual relations even between consenting males illegal, and Wilde was found guilty.

After two short spells in London prisons, Wilde was transferred to Reading Gaol. By now his physical condition had deteriorated, and he was depressed and confused. Impressed by Wilde's reputation as a gifted writer, the prison governor made arrangements for him to work in the garden and in the prison library. But life was still very tough.

If prison's dreary routine was hard for Wilde, things were no better on the outside. His books were withdrawn from sale, his name was removed from theatre posters and he was declared bankrupt. Wilde had been ostracised. On his release, he was philosophical about his time in prison. It had given him time to study himself and there had certainly been long periods of soul-searching – 'that might bring balm to the bruised heart, and peace to the soul in pain', he wrote to Lord Alfred Douglas.

EACH MAN KILLS THE THING HE LOVES

While in prison, Wilde wrote *The Ballad of Reading Gaol* (published in 1898), about a man hanged there for the murder of his wife. This work, more than any other, gave him status as a writer of serious merit.

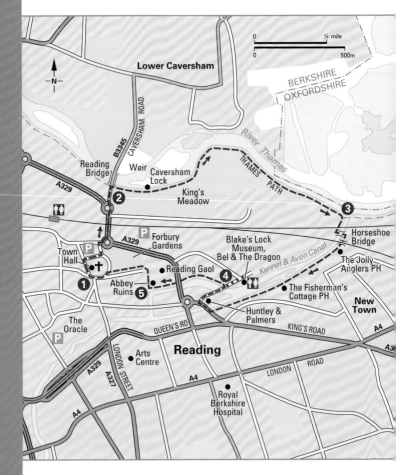

❶ Start by the statue of Queen Victoria. Head the way she is facing, beside the Town Hall, past the entrance to Reading Museum and Art Gallery. Cross Valpy Street and turn right into Forbury Road. Walk down to the roundabout, past the Rising Sun pub on the corner, and turn left towards the railway bridge.

Pass beneath it and cross the road at the pedestrian lights. Cross King's Meadow Road to Reading Bridge.

❷ Take the steps, right, just before the bridge to join the Thames Path. Turn right, heading downstream. Past Caversham Lock the sound of traffic begins to fade and the surroundings become leafier. Skirt King's Meadow, with its smart apartments and houses on the opposite bank. Pass a boatyard full of cabin cruisers and narrowboats, and continue under horse chestnut trees. Eventually reach Kennet Mouth, where a distinctive Sustrans waymarker directs you over the bridge (signed towards Bristol).

❸ Cross the Kennet via Horseshoe Bridge with its distinctive blue-painted wooden slats, and on the far side turn left, back on yourself, heading for central Reading. Pass beneath Brunel's railway bridge, and just past The Fisherman's Cottage note on the opposite bank the picturesque Victorian buildings, formerly Reading's main sewage station, now home to the Riverside Museum (Blake's Lock) and a bar/restaurant. Leave the tow path at the next bridge. Turn right along King's Road, passing the red-brick facade of the old Huntley and Palmer's biscuit factory (look up to see its name), now residential. Turn immediately right, and continue for 100yds (91m) to cross the green-painted bridge built by Reading Gas Company in 1880.

❹ Take a slight detour at this point to follow the signs for the short distance to Blake's Lock. Retrace your steps and turn left onto the tow path, with the huge Prudential building on the left bank. Pass under the King's Road bridge, keep right and follow Chestnut Walk (also known as the Oscar Wilde Memorial Walk). The tall walls of Reading Gaol, where Wilde was imprisoned, are immediately to the right. Adjacent are the rubble-stone ruins of Reading Abbey.

❺ Go up a flight of steps leading to a small garden area. The Abbey ruins are to your right. Go straight through the garden onto Abbot's Walk and ahead of you is Forbury Gardens. Enter these lovely gardens via the main gate opposite the old Abbey Gateway (to the right of here is Reading Crown Court). The centrepiece is a giant statue of a lion, erected to commemorate the late 19th-century imperial campaigns in Afghanistan. Leave the gardens via the Victoria Gate, to the left. Go straight ahead, past the Church of St Laurence-in-Reading on the right, and turn right to return to the start of the walk.

WHERE TO EAT AND DRINK Reading offers numerous pubs, cafe bars, restaurants and hotels. However, on the walk itself you might like to stop off at The Fisherman's Cottage, which overlooks the Kennet and Avon Canal, and enjoy a meal or snack in the pub's conservatory, which has a striking riverside mural. Alternatively, sit outside on a sunny day and enjoy the canal scene. Fresh bread is available daily and there are baguettes to take away.

WHAT TO SEE Blake's Lock Museum is housed in two former industrial buildings, the Screen House and the Turbine House, where displays tell the story of the Kennet and the Thames as they pass through Reading. The highlight is a magnificent gypsy caravan from 1914. Next door, the beautiful ornate brick building of 1873 resembles more a chapel than sewage pumping station. It now houses a stylish bar and restaurant.

WHILE YOU'RE THERE Visit Reading Museum and Art Gallery, which occupies part of the Town Hall. Here you can see a full-size replica of the Bayeux Tapestry, discover artefacts from the Roman town of Silchester, and learn about the history of Huntley and Palmers, Reading's famous biscuit factory. Enquire, too, about access to Reading Abbey grounds.

Overleaf: The River Thames at Pangbourne Meadow (Walk 38)

On the Thames Path at Pangbourne

DISTANCE 3 miles (4.8km)	**MINIMUM TIME** 1hr 30min	

ASCENT/GRADIENT 220ft (67m) ▲▲▲   **LEVEL OF DIFFICULTY** ✚✚✚

PATHS Field and riverside paths, stretches of road, section of Thames Path; several stiles

LANDSCAPE Gentle farmland on banks of Pang and Thames

SUGGESTED MAP AA Walker's Map 24 The Chilterns

START/FINISH Grid reference: SU633765

DOG FRIENDLINESS Lead required in Pangbourne, under control on farmland and by Thames

PARKING Car park off A329 in Pangbourne, near railway bridge

PUBLIC TOILETS At main car park, and at car park on meadow near end of walk

During the Edwardian era the Thames-side settlement of Pangbourne became especially fashionable with artists, writers and anglers, yet apparently it did little to ignite the interest of one renowned literary figure. 'Pleasant house, hate Pangbourne, nothing happens', wrote D H Lawrence in 1919, when he and his wife rented a cottage in the village.

POPULAR PANGBOURNE

On the other hand, D H Evans, who founded the famous West End department store, clearly found Pangbourne to his liking. Towards the end of the 19th century he built seven very distinctive villas in the village. Known as the Seven Deadly Sins and distinguished by domes, turrets, balconies and gables – look for them on the right bank above Whitchurch Lock – the villas were not popular with everyone. There were those who claimed the seven villas had been built to house Evans' seven mistresses, while others believed he lived in a different one each day of the week. Lady Cunard, noted for her notorious parties, bought one of the houses. One local resident claimed the parties were riotous and wild, but added, 'anything would have seemed wild compared to life in Pangbourne'.

The spacious meadows, glorious hanging woods and varied assortment of pubs and hotels have made the village one of the most popular destinations on this stretch of the Thames to this day. The only real changes are a few more shops and a lot more road traffic.

One man whose love for this river lasted a lifetime was Kenneth Grahame. He wrote *The Wind in the Willows* in 1908 and found the inspiration for his delightful story here. Grahame was born in 1859 and first came to live in Berkshire when he was five. His strength lay in his ability to create a magical world for children, providing a fascinating insight into their imagination and their view of the puzzling adult world. Grahame and his wife became parents rather late in life and it was their son's bedtime stories, as well as letters sent to the boy by his father while away on holiday, that formed the basis for Grahame's classic book. Both father and son drew on their love of the Berkshire countryside and its wild creatures to complete the story. Having lived for much of his life in the Thames Valley, Grahame eventually moved to Pangbourne in 1924, buying Church Cottage in the centre of the village. His beloved Thames was only a short walk away, and he died here in 1932.

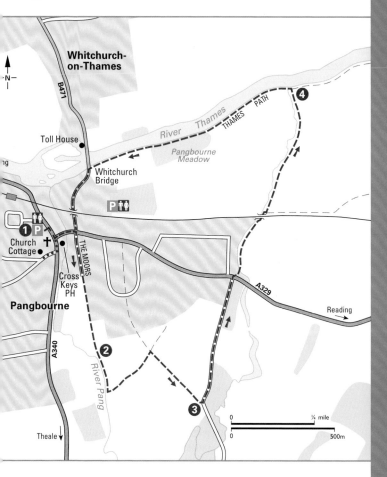

❶ Begin the walk with a very short detour. From the car park turn right to the mini-roundabout, walk along to the church and adjoining Church Cottage (Kenneth Grahame's former home). Retrace your steps to the main road, keep the Cross Keys pub on the right and turn right at the mini-roundabout. Cross the Pang, and immediately past the mini-roundabout on your left, turn right into The Moors. At the end of the drive continue ahead on the footpath. Pass alongside various houses and gardens and patches of scrub, then go through a pretty tunnel of trees. Further on is a gate with a local map and an information board about the area. Beyond the gate the River Pang sweeps in from the right.

❷ Follow the path parallel to the river, with willow trees along the bank. Make for a footbridge but don't cross it. Instead, turn sharp left and walk across the open meadow to a kissing gate in the far boundary. Once over it, keep alongside the hedge on the left. After 100yds (91m), you will see a World War II pill box ahead. Turn right here at a path intersection and cross a footbridge. Continue ahead to a gate with a short footbridge. Go straight across the field and exit left onto the road over a stile.

❸ Follow the lane left between hedges and oak trees and walk along to the A329. Go diagonally right to the footpath by the sign for Purley Rise and follow the path north towards distant trees, a steam on

your left. Go through a kissing gate, turn right and follow the concrete track as it bends left to run beneath the railway line. Once through the tunnel, bear right to a kissing gate and then follow the track along the left edge of the field, beside a rivulet. Ahead on the horizon are glorious hanging woods on the north bank of the Thames. Pass a small concrete bridge to the left (don't cross it) and continue on the footpath as it crosses this gentle lowland landscape. Go through a gate and walk across the next field to reach the riverbank.

❹ On reaching the River Thames, turn left through a gate, cross a footbridge and head towards Pangbourne. Follow the path to Pangbourne Meadow and ahead is Whitchurch Bridge. As you approach it, begin to veer away from the river bank towards a car park (signposted 'public toilets'). Turn right onto a path which leads back to the main road. Turn left, pass beneath the railway line and turn right at the next junction to return to the village centre.

WHERE TO EAT AND DRINK Pangbourne has lots of good pubs and cafes. The Cross Keys is an attractive option, with a patio running down to the River Pang. Or you could buy picnic provisions locally and sit in manicured Pangbourne Meadow in front of Whitchurch Bridge, towards the end of the walk.

WHAT TO SEE Church Cottage, Kenneth Grahame's home, is next door to the Church of St James the Less. The house looks much the same today as it did in Grahame's day, with the little round village lock-up, which he used as a tool shed, in the garden. Towards the end of the walk, as you leave the riverbank, look out for Whitchurch Bridge, a Victorian iron toll bridge, with white lattice architecture. Cars pay to cross the bridge but pedestrians go free.

WHILE YOU'RE THERE Pangbourne's Church of St James the Less is distinguished by its square tower and battlements which tend to dominate the skyline. Kenneth Grahame's funeral took place here in July 1932, and the event was recorded in *The Times*. His body was later moved to Holywell Cemetery in Oxford, where he lies beside his son.

Through Woodlands at Frilsham

DISTANCE 3.5 miles (5.7km)   MINIMUM TIME 1hr 30min

ASCENT/GRADIENT 99ft (30m) ▲▲▲   LEVEL OF DIFFICULTY ✦✦✦

PATHS Tracks, paths and stretches of country road

LANDSCAPE Woodland on northern side of the Pang Valley

SUGGESTED MAP OS Explorer 158 Newbury & Hungerford

START/FINISH Grid reference: SU552730

DOG FRIENDLINESS Under control on Yattendon Estate

PARKING Space at side of The Pot Kiln pub

PUBLIC TOILETS None on route

The story of the English pub spans more than 1,000 years, beginning with the dismal alehouses of the Anglo-Saxon period. Later came the old drovers' hostelries, followed by coaching inns and then Georgian and Victorian pubs built to take advantage of the canal and railway trade. Today our city centres feature themed pubs, dreamed up by marketing whizz-kids, usually designed to appeal to younger drinkers, and many of our country pubs have gone down the dining route. With changing population patterns, declining pub drinks consumption, and the problem of drinking and driving, many hostelries have had little choice other than to become upmarket dining pubs. Sadly many of these are now effectively mere restaurants with a bar attached, a shadow of their former selves in terms of character and history.

A TRADITIONAL LOCAL

The Pot Kiln has been a famous tavern in this isolated part of West Berkshire for decades. Until the beginning of World War II there were brick kilns in this area – hence the name of the pub. From the outside the inn could almost pass for a farm or a private house, and secluded among trees, it is superbly located down a narrow country lane. It used to be notoriously hard to find – it is not in the village centre, so when you are close by, don't turn off to follow the Frilsham sign, instead look for the (approriate) brown heritage signpost.

There have been many additions and various changes to the inn over the years, and it too has succumbed, in part, to 'dining-pub syndrome'. Its bar, however, retains its original character. On a summer's day sitting in its front garden, gazing out over nothing but glorious countryside while enjoying a glass or two of the splendid real ales it serves, is still an unbeatable pub experience in the finest English tradition.

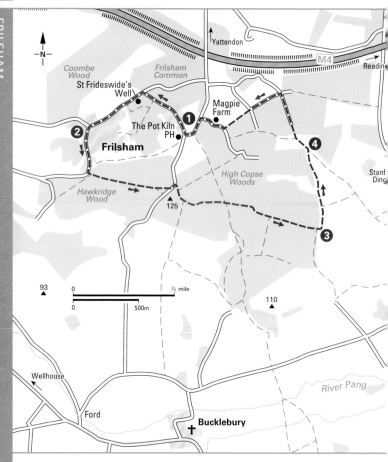

① With The Pot Kiln and then its stables on your left, follow the track into the woods, passing several houses, including Laurel Bank Cottages. Ignore the public footpath on the left, go past two cottages and bear left just beyond them to follow a footpath between holly trees. This leads to a turning, on the left, to St Frideswide's Well. It is dedicated to the semi-legendary French saint (as is Frilsham Church), who may have visited these parts in the late 7th century. Local lore has it that young couples would come to the well to see if the male was approved of by a spitting toad that lived here. If the creature spat at him, then it was

assumed that his intentions were not honourable. Return to the path, bear right at the next fork and continue straight on to the road. Turn left and walk through Frilsham village. Pass Beechfield, a residential development, and turn left at the sign for Hermitage and Bucklebury.

② Beyond Little Orchard, where the lane bends right, go straight ahead, following the path deep into the woods. Pass through a gate and continue on the bridleway to the next waymarker. Turn left at this point, following the path down the wooded slope to the road. Cross over, walk left downhill for 100yds (91m), then turn right onto a track signed 'Restricted Byway'. Pass a waymarked track on the right and continue on the main track, following it through woodland to the next waymarked junction.

③ Turn left here and cut through bluebell woods to a gate. Cross the field to a fence gap in the next boundary, with traffic on the M4 visible in the distance. Veer half left in the field. To the right in the distance you can just make out the facade of Yattendon Court, up among the trees. Cross the field and make for a bridleway gate on the right, running into the trees.

④ Beyond the wood, follow the path between fences and swing left at the next waymarked junction. Walk along the track to the next junction, where there are footpath and bridleway signs, and veer right. Follow the track round the side of Magpie Farm and on reaching the road, turn left. Return to the car park by The Pot Kiln.

WHERE TO EAT AND DRINK The Pot Kiln serves highly acclaimed, if rather pricey, gastropub food at lunchtimes and in the evenings. It specialises in game and wild food, sourced locally, as are many of its salad and vegetables, picked daily from the kitchen garden. Beware that The Pot Kiln closes all day Tuesday, and on other weekdays keeps traditional hours, closing at 2.30pm and reopening at 6pm.

WHAT TO SEE The Yattendon Estate supplies Christmas trees to places from Land's End to John o'Groats, and with more than 1.8 million trees planted over 600 acres (243ha), it is one of Britain's biggest producers. Around 150,000 Christmas trees are sold here every year. Walking through the estate reveals the sheer scale and size of the operation.

WHILE YOU'RE THERE The West Berkshire Brewery set up in 1995 as a microbrewery, initially located at The Pot Kiln. It has now moved to Yattendon, just the other side of the M4 from Frilsham, and has since become a 'local hero', winning dozens of awards for its beers and catering for many pubs and other outlets all over Berkshire and beyond. Brewery tours take place monthly and must be booked online.

From Bucklebury to Stanford Dingley

DISTANCE 4.5 miles (7.2km)		MINIMUM TIME 1hr 30 min	

ASCENT/GRADIENT 95ft (29m) ▲▲▲   LEVEL OF DIFFICULTY ✦✦✦

PATHS Tracks, grassy paths, fields, riverside path and stretches of country road; several stiles

LANDSCAPE Woods and fields on northern side of Pang Valley

SUGGESTED MAP OS Explorer 158 Newbury & Hungerford

START/FINISH Grid reference: SU552709

DOG FRIENDLINESS Under control

PARKING Car park beside recreation ground in Bucklebury

PUBLIC TOILETS None on route

The sleepy village of Bucklebury first hit world popular press headlines in November 2010 as the family home of Catherine Elizabeth 'Kate' Middleton, Prince William's bride-to-be. And in July 2013 it was back to the family home in Bucklebury that the Duchess of Cambridge, as she had now become, brought her newborn son George. It was reported that the royal couple were desperate to swap the attention of London and the formality of their royal home, Kensington Palace, for somewhere they felt welcome and more at home. Whether they will still be allowed by the world's press (or their own security staff) to do the 'normal' things they used to do, such as enjoy a quiet drink at The Old Boot Inn at Stanford Dingley, is quite a different matter.

FIT FOR A PRINCESS

A 'commoner' Kate may be, but she will hardly want for much whenever she chooses to return to the country village where she grew up. The family house, Bucklebury Manor, is a Grade II-listed Georgian home, set in 18 acres (7.5ha) with tennis court, swimming pool and library. The village is not reticent about its meteoric rise to fame and was quick to point out that not one but two future kings were staying with them (even if only for a short while). One enterprising local shop, having previously sold commemorative Kate and William wedding mugs, produced a special edition to celebrate the birth of Prince George, and promptly sold its initial batch of 500. Not to be outdone, Bucklebury Parish Council commissioned a limited edition 'Hooray for George' mug.

On a more monumental scale, there are plans to install a set of grand gates which will commemorate the marriage of Kate and William and the birth of Prince George. Meanwhile Bucklebury councillors are also keen to enlist the services of a local sculptor to create a piece of public art and/or erect an ornamental village sign on the green. Whatever happens, Bucklebury will never quite be the same – nor, probably, would it want to be.

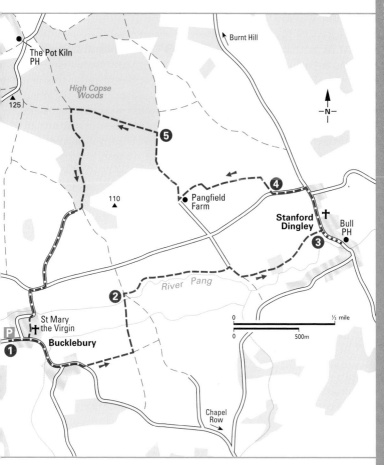

❶ Cross the road from the car park to the church. Make your way to the side door and leave the churchyard to the left-hand side of the lovely timber-framed cottage. Turn left and continue on the road for a while. Eventually, on the right-hand side of the road you come to a fine old red-brick building which used to be the school house (unsigned). Opposite here, take the right of way on the left. Follow a grassy track, and three-quarters of the way across

a field, reach the corner of a ditch and a waymarker. Turn left and head for a footbridge and stile. Continue ahead in the next field and make for a bridge, crossing it.

❷ Turn right to follow the River Pang to Stanford Dingley. Keep straight ahead on a grassy waterside path, eventually reaching two stiles, a gate and a track. Bear right here for 80yds (73m) to the next gateway, swinging left immediately before it. Keep left as the path forks, making for a kissing gate among the trees in the far corner. Cross a footbridge and go through a wood to the next kissing gate, and then follow the path across the pasture, keeping Stanford Dingley Church in view. Make for a stile at the road and turn right to make the short detour to the Bull.

3 Retrace your steps, go past the church and head away from the village to a staggered junction. Take the first left turning, following the road back to Bucklebury for a short distance. (Make sure that you do not continue straight ahead at this point as the Bucklebury signposting is ambiguous.)

4 As the road begins to curve left, look for a path and stile on the right and enter the field. Follow the boundary to a stile and walk ahead across the next field, aiming to the right of Pangfield Farm. As you draw level with the outbuildings, take the path on the right. Join the right of way further along and follow it between trees and then through the woodland. Keep ahead to the next waymarked junction.

5 Turn left here and continue deep into High Copse Woods. As you continue, piles of logs can often be seen lining the route, waiting to be transported to sawmills. After 650yds (594m) take the waymarked path left downhill for a similar distance until you get to a pretty timber-framed house. Join the drive and walk for another 600yds (549m) down to the road. Turn right, then take the next left turn back towards Bucklebury. Cross the River Pang over a small humpback bridge and go straight ahead. Go through a kissing gate, across the field and exit via another kissing gate to return to the church and the car park.

WHERE TO EAT AND DRINK The Bull at Stanford Dingley serves gastro-pub food. The building dates back to the 15th century and includes a wealth of original timbers as well as the remains of an original wattle-and-daub wall. One of its more unusual features is the traditional (and now quite rare) pub game known as ring-the-bull, involving a genuine surviving bull's ring.

WHAT TO SEE Bucklebury village's Church of St Mary the Virgin was originally built in the second half of the 11th century and retains its ornate Norman south doorway. Kate and William attended the annual Christmas service here in 2012 and joined the locals singing traditional carols.

WHILE YOU'RE THERE If the grand gates to commemorate the marriage of Kate and William get the go-ahead they will be sited at the entrance to The Avenue, a sweeping road that leads to tree-lined Bucklebury Common (south of the village). In a neat royal twist this was planted with saplings – now mighty oaks – to mark a visit by Queen Elizabeth I in the 16th century.

Around Douai Abbey

DISTANCE 3 miles (4.8km)	MINIMUM TIME 1hr 30min

ASCENT/GRADIENT 90ft (27m) ▲▲▲   LEVEL OF DIFFICULTY ✚✚✚

PATHS Tracks, field and woodland paths, stretches of village road and country lane

LANDSCAPE Mixture of woodland and farmland on south-facing slopes of the Kennet Valley

SUGGESTED MAP OS Explorer 159 Reading, Wokingham & Pangbourne

START/FINISH Grid reference: SU589688

DOG FRIENDLINESS On lead in Beenham, near Douai and near livestock, under control on woodland stretches

PARKING Small car park by Victory Hall

PUBLIC TOILETS None on route, but enquire at Abbey reception

The Douai Abbey community covers more than three and a half centuries. The Dissolution of the Monasteries during the reign of Henry VIII drove men and women who opted for a monastic existence to flee abroad. In 1615 a group of English monks gathered in Paris to form the community of St Edmund. Other English monasteries were formed, and together they restored the English Benedictine Congregation. Having been suppressed and almost extinguished by the events of the French Revolution, the survivors of St Edmund's moved, in 1818, to Douai, some 25 miles (40km) south of Lille. In 1903 the monks were again expelled from their monastery on anti-clerical grounds.

THE MONKS RETURN

This time they crossed the Channel, bringing the name 'Douai' with them. The monks were welcomed by the Bishop of Portsmouth who allowed them to settle at Woolhampton, taking over the parish and St Mary's College school. They went on to transform the latter into one of the country's leading Roman Catholic public schools, until its eventual closure in 1999.

A NEW ABBEY

Work on the new abbey building began in 1928 according to a design by Arnold Crush, which can be seen in the choir and sanctuary areas. The initial plan was to have a transept crossing surmounted by a tower, and with another seven bays the church would have extended almost to the road. However it took five years alone before the traditional-looking east end, constructed in a style that reflected the continuity of monastic architecture from the Benedictine Middle Ages, was completed. In fact, it took until the summer of 1993 and a change of architect (in 1987 Dr Michael Blee was invited to start work on a new design), before the church was completed and dedicated in a style that suited the modern monastic age, with the focus on prayer and praise.

These days the Douai community includes around 30 monks, who receive guests, host conferences and offer a place of retreat. They help organise events in the church itself and in other parts of the abbey campus, as well as working in the surrounding parish.

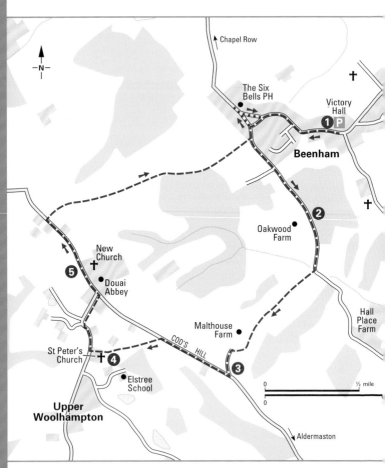

❶ From the car park turn right and follow the main road through Beenham; this changes its name several times, becoming Picklepythe Lane for a stretch, past the recreation ground, to Clay Lane. Veer left and left again by The Willows. Follow the byway (ignore all footpath signs) and eventually pass the two brick pillars that mark the entrance to Oakwood Farm.

❷ Continue downhill through a natural tunnel of trees. Some 100yds (91m) after you've emerged back into the light, where the trail swings left turn right at the bridleway sign. Follow it to the left along the field perimeter, steadily climbing to the top of the field. At the top Malthouse Farm is on your right. Continue on this rough byway to meet the road, with a paved drive leading off to your right to Malthouse Farm.

❸ Turn right and walk along the main road, Cod's Hill (a corruption of God's Hill), leading to the abbey. Take the first footpath on the left, which almost immediately crosses a drive and seems to disappear. Look to the left of the barbed wire fence and the path continues through a gap, across Douai Park playing fields. Head towards the white cricket pavilion, and look to the left for the kissing gate into the churchyard of St Peter's, Woolhampton (hidden behind trees). Look right for your first view of Douai Abbey.

❹ Visit the church, then exit right, out of the gate back onto the road. As the road nears the bend, take the path which runs parallel to the road and continue as far as the main road, opposite the main entrance to the old part of Douai Abbey. Bear left

here, with the Abbey buildings on your right and a row of late 17th-century thatched cottages to your left. The older red-brick buildings of Douai are not open to the public (the old church may be visited by appointment), but continue along the road to Douai Abbey where you can visit the new church.

❺ Beyond the church, continue along the road to some cottages and barns. Turn right at a footpath sign, soon passing a galvanised gate, and follow the track round to the left into the next field. Keep to the field-edge, and when you reach the corner by the footpath sign, go straight over into the woods. Fields can be seen close by on the left. Follow the path through the trees, then between paddocks, until you reach the track that you took near the start of the walk. To return to your car turn left, then right by Jayswood Cottage, and right again to the main road. Alternatively, go left by Jayswood Cottage, turn left at the junction, and The Six Bells pub is just a few paces away on the other side of the road.

WHERE TO EAT AND DRINK The Six Bells lies in the centre of Beenham, near the end (or if you like, the start) of the walk. It has a good selection of real ales and an extensive menu.

WHAT TO SEE Next to Woolhampton Church lie the buildings of Elstree School, a famous preparatory school that includes novelist Sebastian Faulks and singer James Blunt among its former pupils.

WHILE YOU'RE THERE St Peter's Church at Woolhampton was completely Gothicised in the mid-19th century. The roof and main walls of the old church were retained and the walls encased in flint. The old bell tower was also transformed into an attractive shingled spire.

Wasing Park and Brimpton

DISTANCE 6 miles (9.7km)	MINIMUM TIME 2hrs 30min

ASCENT/GRADIENT 150ft (46m) ▲▲▲   LEVEL OF DIFFICULTY ✦✦✦

PATHS Field and woodland paths and tracks, parkland drives, meadow, road and riverside; many stiles

LANDSCAPE Common, parkland, woodland and meadow

SUGGESTED MAP OS Explorer 159 Reading, Wokingham & Pangbourne

START/FINISH Grid reference: SU567628

DOG FRIENDLINESS Lead required in Wasing Park

PARKING Limited spaces opposite The Pineapple pub

PUBLIC TOILETS None on route

Berkshire, like Buckinghamshire, is blessed with many fine villages that, thankfully, have stood the test of time and remained largely intact. While some have fallen victim to planning blight and seen their boundaries expanded in recent years, others have successfully fought off late 20th-century development, their pride and spirit intact.

A SURVIVOR

One such village that has so far avoided change is Brimpton, just to the south of the A4, between Newbury and Reading. Bounded to the north by the River Kennet and to the south by the lesser-known River Enborne, Brimpton, in the main, lies at the end of a breezy ridge. As a village it's like hundreds of others around the country, b it is that similarity that makes it a typical English rural community. Look closely and you'll see that its key component parts remain in place – the shop and post office, the public house, the primary school and the church are all here.

Village records reveal a fascinating insight into how Brimpton has evolved over the years into the community you see today. As with most rural settlements, Brimpton was once part of the feudal system, shaped and controlled by landowning families, aristocrats and local benefactors. In 1854 the Countess of Falmouth built almshouses for elderly couples and widows, while the Earl donated a small piece of land on which to build a school. Later, when the church was rebuilt, local squire James Blyth objected to the pub being near the church and gave land for a new site.

Between Brimpton and Brimpton Common lies the 4,000-acre (1608ha) Wasing Estate, established in 1759 and under the stewardship of the same family ever since. The heart of the estate is the small

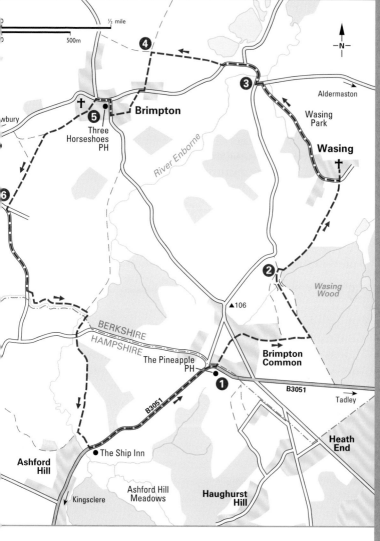

complex of buildings known as Wasing Park. Clustered around the simple yet lovely Church of St Nicholas, largely rebuilt in 1761, are tall trees and several beautifully restored ancient buildings. Charming Wasing Park is now used to host wedding ceremonies.

❶ Follow the path opposite The Pineapple across two stiles to the road. Cross over to join a byway, and follow it round to the right and across the common. When it swings sharp left, go straight on along the public footpath, still a track. Take the path to the right of Woodside, bear left

at a T-junction (signed 'Permitted Bridleway') and follow the path. Where it joins a track, veer off left at a waymarker, following the field-edge path. Just past the corner of the field veer to your right and follow a narrow path (this may be overgrown). Look for an opening in the trees ahead, cross a bridge, and continue as the path goes down then up, and turns right at a track. At the first junction go right, following the battered old sign 'For visiting (Wasing) church and graveyard only'. (If you reach a tarmac lane you have missed the right turn and will have to go back.)

2 Pass a kissing gate, take the track, turn left at the bend and cut through the wood. Go through the gate signed 'Private Wasing Estate', and the small complex of buildings known as Wasing Park is directly ahead. Cross a track, go through a kissing gate, then through a field to visit the church via another kissing gate. Return to the drive. Turn right and pass between gate piers and continue ahead at crossroads, over a cattle grid. Follow the drive down to the road beyond a gate and a lodge.

3 Bear left to a junction, then right over the River Enborne to a fork. Keep left onto Wasing Road and turn right at the 'Wasing Estate Shalford Lakes' sign. Go through a gate, with the lakes over your right shoulder, to veer left along a grassy track, following the edge of the field (Brimpton Church is visible to your left). Make towards the houses to a junction, and turn left by a galvanised gate.

4 Follow the path to the road and turn right. After a few paces go left to join the next path. Keep over to the left edge of the field, go through a kissing gate in the top corner and veer right. Turn right almost immediately you are through the next kissing gate to reach a housing estate. Turn right at the road, pass the Three Horseshoes pub and walk along to the church, following the waymarked path around the pretty churchyard.

5 The path leads into fields from the top left-hand corner of the churchyard. Just beneath the second set of power lines turn left, with a tall transmission mast on the horizon directly ahead. Head south to Hyde End Lane via three gates.

6 Turn left, keeping right at the fork onto a stony track, and passing entrances to The Lodge and Hyde End House. Look for a stile to the left of a footbridge and cross a meadow. Over the stile, follow the river bank to a footbridge and stile. Cross over and take the path through the wood to a brick bridge. Cross the road and follow the track, taking the path to the left of it between the woodland edge and wire fence. Cross a stile and plank bridge, and make for a bridge in the far right corner of the field. Follow a line of trees to a stile and cross the next pasture towards buildings. Approaching a gate and a cottage, veer left to a stile. Cross to another stile by the road, opposite The Ship Inn. Turn left here and walk along the road (B3051) back to The Pineapple.

WHERE TO EAT AND DRINK The Pineapple, at the start and finish, is a picturesque thatched pub. Inside are low ceilings, quarry tiled floors, beams and fireplaces. The Three Horseshoes at Brimpton is a village local.

WHAT TO SEE Fans of the popular BBC television series *Cranford* may recognise Wasing Park, part of which was the location for The Glebe. The original book was set in Cheshire, but all the outdoor scenes for the TV series were shot in locations across southern England, including Dorney Court (see Walk 24) and Hambleden (see Walk 20).

Hermitage and Little Hungerford

DISTANCE 6 miles (9.7km)	MINIMUM TIME 2hrs 45min

ASCENT/GRADIENT 320ft (98m) ▲▲▲　　LEVEL OF DIFFICULTY ✦✦✦

PATHS Field and woodland paths and tracks, some road; several stiles

LANDSCAPE Extensive woodland with areas of open farmland

SUGGESTED MAP OS Explorer 158 Newbury & Hungerford

START/FINISH Grid reference: SU505730

DOG FRIENDLINESS Under control in woods and on lead near livestock

PARKING Limited parking in Hermitage

PUBLIC TOILETS None on route

One of Britain's most famous and most outspoken 20th-century writers lived quietly in a Berkshire village at the end of World War I. He came here in unusual circumstances and deliberately chose a low profile.

LOCAL SUSPICION

During the early years of the war, David Herbert Lawrence (1885–1930) and his bride, Frieda, lived near St Ives in Cornwall. Frieda was German – and living among people who had lost, and were still losing loved ones in the terrible battles of the Great War, meant she was never going to be accepted by the local community. To make matters worse, Lawrence was a pacifist and, contrary to the fashionable opinions of the day, openly opposed the war. Ill health gave him a genuine reason not to fight, but his outspoken views and choice of bride hardly endeared him to either the villagers or the authorities. Lawrence was ordered to leave the town.

The couple moved to Hermitage, near Newbury, in December 1917, renting a small cottage from a friend. It was a quiet, out-of-the-way kind of place, but even here they were not left alone. While living at Chapel Farm Cottage, they received regular calls from the police.

WALKING AND WRITING

Despite still being harassed, Lawrence enjoyed life in Berkshire and particularly liked walking in the immediate area. He was able to combine his knowledge of the countryside with his skill as a writer, using prose and imagery to convey his love of creation. A keen artist and gardener, Lawrence would also write at great speed, and it was while living at what is now called Warborough Cottage that he undertook some revision of earlier work, including *Women in Love* (1921). During the two years he lived at the cottage Lawrence worked on various short stories, several novels and some poetry. Of all his writing, the story most closely associated with Hermitage is 'The Fox', first published in 1923 in *Three Novellas*. The story is set at Bailey Farm, which Lawrence based on Grimsbury Farm, just outside the village. The setting including the nearby railway are all faithfully recreated, while the nearby market town is undoubtedly Newbury.

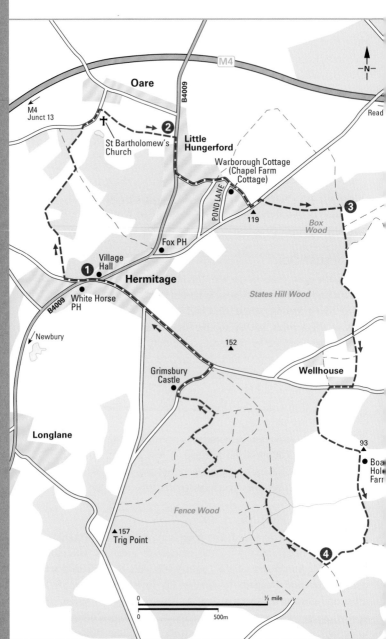

1 With Hermitage Village Hall at your back, turn right, then first right into Doctors Lane. Cross a stile by a private road sign and head across the field to the next stile. Pass beneath power lines and make for a kissing gate in the boundary of the woodland ahead. Take the left fork and follow the footpath through the trees as far as a cottage to your left. Turn left when you reach the track, go past the cottage entrance, and veer right after 100yds (91m) at a public footpath sign onto a narrow path (which may be overgrown). This drops sharply down through woodland to a lane. Turn right and walk along the lane to the hamlet of Oare. Go past its church and turn right into a lane with a small pond on your left.

2 Go through a waymarked side gate and continue alongside a hedge. Leave the field at Little Hungerford and turn right onto the road beside a school. Turn left into Chapel Lane and follow the road round the right-hand bend. Pass Deacon Lane, then Pond Lane. Lawrence's former home, now called Warborough Cottage, is on the corner as you head for the next road junction; its front entrance is in Pond Lane and its rear garden backs onto Chapel Lane. At the main road turn left, then almost immediately right onto a public footpath leading into Box Wood. Cross a stile and follow the track straight ahead deep into the wood until you eventually reach a waymarked post (green-and-white man symbol), immediately before a bridleway.

3 Turn right here and follow the (sometimes very muddy) track through the trees, keeping left at a fork, to eventually reach a road. Cross over by a bungalow and continue on the next section of track. Turn right at the next road and walk along to the turning for Boar's Hole Farm, left. Follow the track to the farm and continue to a sharp left-hand bend. Go through the gate, right, and make for a gate and house in the field corner. Keep to the right of the house, via a gate, then turn right at a track bend and crossroads, passing through a galvanised metal gate onto a restricted byway.

4 Follow the woodland track and keep right at the fork. Cross a stream and pass a left turning. Take the next left path by a stream and pass over a staggered junction. Turn right by the pond, then first left, cutting through the trees. Swing right at the next junction and follow the track as it keeps climbing. Now within the ramparts of ancient Grimsbury Castle, keep left at the junction and make for the road by the castellated cottage. Turn right and walk along to the road junction. Bear left and return to Hermitage.

WHERE TO EAT AND DRINK Hermitage has two pubs – the Fox and the White Horse. Both are typical village locals offering a range of beers and pub food.

WHAT TO SEE Grimsbury Castle is a hill-fort with its origins in the years preceding the Roman conquest. A notice board explains its history. Probably only the expert eye will spot what remains of ramp, ditch and counterscarp bank, but you can't miss the charming castellated 18th-century folly house.

WHILE YOU'RE THERE Stop and look at St Bartholomew's Church at Oare, built on the site of a priory chapel. The history of Oare, from AD 968, is described inside. The present building dates from 1852.

Snelsmore Common to Donnington Castle

DISTANCE 3.5 miles (5.7km)   MINIMUM TIME 1hr 45min

ASCENT/GRADIENT 165ft (50m) ▲▲▲   LEVEL OF DIFFICULTY ✦✦✦

PATHS Paths and tracks through woods

LANDSCAPE Formal country park and woodland

SUGGESTED MAP OS Explorer 158 Newbury & Hungerford

START/FINISH Grid reference: SU463709

DOG FRIENDLINESS Under control at Snelsmore Common (lead required during nesting season, March to June) and by golf course

PARKING Car park at Snelsmore Common Country Park

PUBLIC TOILETS Snelsmore Common Country Park

On a hillside to the north of Newbury lie the ruins of Donnington Castle, once a major stronghold commanding the key routes through the town (now the A4 and the A34). The castle's great strategic importance was underlined by the prolonged fighting for it during the Civil War. Today what remains looks down, somewhat forlornly, on a town that has spread widely since those days.

A LONG HISTORY

The manor of Deritone (now Donnington) was held by the Crown in 1086. In 1386 Richard II granted a licence to 'build anew' and crenellate Donnington Castle to Sir Richard de Abberbury, a former guardian of the King. Later the castle passed to Thomas Chaucer, probably the son of the poet. By the time of Elizabeth I it was back in royal possession – there are accounts of restoration work to the castle in preparation for her visit there in 1568. This included planking the bridge, mending chamber floors, building sheds for the kitchen and making tables and trestles.

CIVIL WAR

At the time of the Civil War, Donnington Castle belonged to John Packer, whose refusal of a loan to the King and opposition in Parliament led to the confiscation of his property by Charles I. After the First Battle of Newbury in September 1643, Colonel John Boys was sent to take command of the castle for the King, with 200 foot soldiers, 25 horses and four cannons. He strengthened the defences by constructing a star fort earthworks around it, which can still be seen below the castle. Boys withstood two Parliamentary assaults on the castle in July and September 1644, and was knighted by the King in October.

The Second Battle of Newbury, on 27 October 1644, was somewhat inconclusive, but the Royalist army was able to slip away leaving the crown, the Great Seal and artillery in Boys' keeping at Donnington. Boys then withstood another siege by the Parliamentary army, until relieved by the King on 9 November. Repeated attempts were made to take the castle, but Boys did not surrender until instructed to do so by the King on 1 April 1646.

The outline of the castle can still be traced, though only the impressive twin-towered, 14th-century gatehouse has survived intact. The castle hill is open freely, and the short climb is well worth the effort to admire not only the building but also the panoramic views.

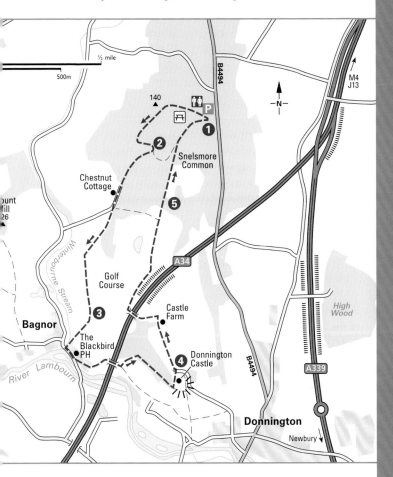

1 With the car park height restriction barrier immediately behind you, veer right and continue through the car park. Follow the paved track through two sets of gates (usually open) to a kissing gate. Beyond this the track curves gradually to the left, then runs clear and straight to a left curve. Pass a seat, then a path on the right, and continue for a few paces to a bridleway (signed 'byway').

2 Turn sharp right and veer half left at the next fork, ignoring the path sharp left. Keep straight on, passing to the right of both the first and second wooden seats, then take the left fork to descend the steep bank, through bracken, reaching a galvanised gate at the bottom. Go through it and follow the path, which becomes a track. Pass Chestnut Cottage, and go straight ahead when the track bends right. Follow the long path along the woodland edge. Eventually you will see a golf course on the left. Reach a wooden kissing gate on the right, and go through it.

3 Head down the grassy field slope towards the houses of Bagnor. Go through the gate, and at the road turn left, passing The Blackbird pub (see Walk 45). Go past the front of its garden and continue on the gravelled track past houses. Go left past Foxgrove through a kissing gate, and take the tarmac path which goes up and over the A34 via a bridge, to a golf course. Keep left (straight on) at the fork on the far side of the footbridge, heading towards the woodland. Cross the drive, and just to the left is a sign, 'Top Barn Access'. Opposite this on the right-hand side follow the waymarked path, which threads through the trees. Emerge from the woods at a gate, go through it, and climb the short, steep slope up to Donnington Castle.

4 With the entrance to the gatehouse at your back, look left for a wooden gate. Go through this. It leads to a track, where you turn left. Pass between the timber barns of Castle Farm, then bear left down a tarmac bridleway. Re-cross the A34 and sweep right along the bridleway, following the drive which dwindles to a track. Keep right at the fork and cut between fences. On the left are broad fairways. Follow the track towards a house set against the trees. The path runs around to the left of it.

5 Pass through a gate onto Snelsmore Common and go straight ahead at the waymarked junction. Pass beneath power lines and continue between bracken and gorse bushes. Keep right (straight on) at the next fork and follow the waymarker pointing towards the car park. Pass the wooden observation tower, veer right onto another path as they merge and pass a small car park. Within sight of the road, look for a stile on the left which returns to the car park entrance.

WHERE TO EAT AND DRINK Snelsmore Common Country Park is ideal for a picnic; hot and cold drinks and food are sold at the Country Store shop in the car park. If you prefer a pub, The Blackbird at Bagnor has a nice garden and offers a menu of simple pub dishes.

WHAT TO SEE As you gaze out from the hill of Donnington Castle, look straight ahead to the buildings of Speen and then far right to Wash Common, which covers part of the site of the First Battle of Newbury. This was a defining moment in the Civil War – principally a missed opportunity for the Royalists to effectively crush the Parliamentarian rebellion.

WHILE YOU'RE THERE Explore the heathland and woods of Snelsmore Common Country Park. Between May and September you are likely to see Dexter cattle – one of the older breeds, and the smallest of all European cattle (about half to one-third the size of a traditional Hereford or Friesian cow). These are grazed on the common to help control tree and scrub invasion.

Through the Lambourn Valley from Bagnor

DISTANCE 3 miles (4.8km)	**MINIMUM TIME** 1hr 30min

ASCENT/GRADIENT 82ft (25m) ▲▲▲　　**LEVEL OF DIFFICULTY** +++

PATHS Grassy paths, paved tracks and woodland paths, some road walking; several stiles

LANDSCAPE Woodland, farmland and riverside

SUGGESTED MAP OS Explorer 158 Newbury & Hungerford

START/FINISH Grid reference: SU455695

DOG FRIENDLINESS Under control near Watermill Theatre and by river near waterfowl

PARKING Patrons welcome to use car park at The Blackbird pub (or Watermill Theatre)

PUBLIC TOILETS None on route

The name Lambourn means 'stream where lambs are washed', and the valley's historic prosperity has been due in large part to sheep, which you will still see grazing in the fields on this walk. The River Lambourn is a sparkling chalk stream, filtered to a rare clarity and fertility by rock laid down 100 million years ago. Now classified as a Site of Special Scientific Interest, the river appears up and down the valley according to rainfall – unusually in modern times its flow is near-natural, largely unchanged by groundwater abstraction. It has a single perennial tributary, the Winterbourne Stream, which joins it at the unspoiled hamlet of Bagnor (see Walk 44), which is intrinsically linked to the river. In fact Bagnor means 'riverbank frequented by badgers' in Anglo-Saxon. You will be lucky to see badgers here now but the village, sustained by watercress beds, the mill, and the Manor Farm until recent times, has hardly changed over the last century.

A CONVERTED WATERMILL

The Lambourn is particularly beautiful where it flows through the grounds of the Watermill Theatre in Bagnor; here you might spot kingfishers – a flash of electric blue – or, more likely, herons. The original mill on the site is mentioned in the Domesday Book, but the present incarnation dates back only to the 1820s. It has been used as a fulling mill (for the beating and cleaning of cloth in water), a paper mill, and probably became a corn mill in the 1850s. In the 1960s it was magnificently restored and converted to become a privately owned repertory theatre. It retains many of its original architectural features, including its waterwheel, which may be viewed through a screen on entry to the auditorium.

Despite the fact its stage is small and it can only hold an audience of 220 people, the theatre is acknowledged as one of England's finest regional playhouses, and is one of only five to have been awarded a National Touring remit by Arts Council England. Many shows produced here transfer to the West End and/or tour throughout the UK or overseas. Successful actors who have begun their careers at the Watermill include Sean Bean, Bill Nighy and David Suchet.

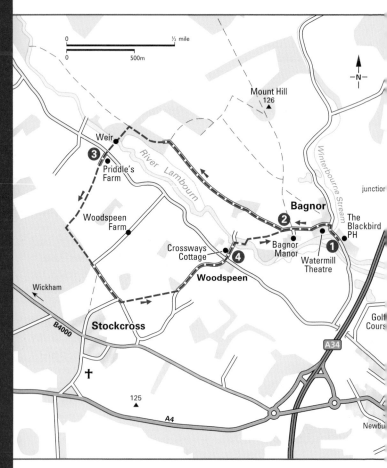

❶ With The Blackbird pub at your back, turn right along the beautifully planted main street, cross the Winterbourne Stream and turn left to pay a visit to the Watermill Theatre. Come out of the theatre, turn left back onto the main road, then fork

next left to follow the drive towards the gates of Bagnor Manor. Follow the track as it heads to the right of the house, past a traffic mirror on the left and a bridleway on the right. Go over a stile and continue ahead to another stile.

2 Do not cross the second stile. Instead swing right and follow a long, straight grassy stretch between tall hedgerows, with the farmland of Bagnor Manor to your left. Eventually the track curves gently to the right by a grove of trees. Just past an overgrown stile and open field on the right, the trail runs through a dense copse. As you emerge from the woodland, turn left at the waymark, and after a few paces cross the concrete bridge over the River Lambourn. Turn right, taking the path by the meadow. Cross a weir and bridge to a kissing gate, continue up a flight of steps and out to the road.

3 Cross over and follow the byway ahead, to the right of Priddle's Farm. After a steep start it continues with views left to horse paddocks, then fields and eventually panoramic views. After it bends left, go past the entrance to Woodspeen Farm, past the footpath right to Stockcross Jubilee Wood, and continue to the road on a bend at Rookwood. Swing left at this point to join a byway, following the sunken path as it descends to Snake Lane (muddy when wet). Bear left and walk to the road junction. Cross over and follow the waymarked lane, swinging right to a footbridge when you reach Crossways Cottage.

4 Follow the pretty but narrow and muddy riverside path. Cross two bridges to a stile and continue between fields and fences to the next stile. The spectacular dovecote on the right belongs to Bagnor Manor. Continue ahead along the drive and turn right, retracing your steps to the centre of Bagnor village.

WHERE TO EAT AND DRINK Time your visit to coincide with a performance at the Watermill Theatre and call in for a matinee lunch, cream tea, or early evening food and drink (booking advisable). A riverside drink in summer here is idyllic. Bagnor's unpretentious village pub, The Blackbird, has a nice garden and offers a reasonable menu.

WHAT TO SEE Next to the Watermill Theatre is Rack Marsh Nature Reserve, freely open to the public. It's a fine example of a wet meadow, characteristic of the Lambourn valley in days gone by. It's full of rushes and sedges, and its flora includes early marsh-orchids, bogbeans, marsh-marigolds and water avens; birders may spot blackcaps, chiffchaffs, grey herons, kingfishers, reed and sedge warblers, and whitethroats.

WHILE YOU'RE THERE If you're interested in the history of the English Civil War, or would simply like to extend this walk and enjoy a terrific hilltop view next to a splendid medieval gatehouse, stroll west for around 0.5 miles (800m) from The Blackbird pub, across the A34, to Donnington Castle (see Walk 44).

From Thatcham across Greenham Common

DISTANCE 6.5 miles (10.4km)   MINIMUM TIME 2hrs 30min

ASCENT/GRADIENT Negligible ▲▲▲   LEVEL OF DIFFICULTY ✚✚✚

PATHS Canal tow path, tracks, common paths, roads

LANDSCAPE Valley rising to wooded commons

SUGGESTED MAP OS Explorer 158 Newbury & Hungerford

START/FINISH Grid reference: SU527663

DOG FRIENDLINESS Lead required at Crookham and Greenham commons during bird-breeding season; under control on canal tow path

PARKING Thatcham Station

PUBLIC TOILETS Newbury town

NOTES This walk requires a return by train to Thatcham from Newbury – check train times ahead

Greenham Common's former airbase is synonymous with CND rallies, women's protest groups and cruise missiles – a powerful evocation of the Cold War period and the threat of nuclear attack. Today the derelict buildings have been demolished and the 9-mile (14.5km) perimeter fence – once famously encircled by 30,000 women protestors holding hands – has been removed. Only the air traffic control tower remains.

A MILITARY AIR BASE

An area of open common land, Greenham was acquired by the Air Ministry in 1941 for use as a military base, home to British squadrons and then the US Air Force. In 1951 the Americans set about building the longest military runway in Europe here, and in 1983 the first (of 96) nuclear-armed cruise missiles arrived, making Greenham Common a focus of world attention for the rest of that decade. Thankfully the Intermediate-Range Nuclear Forces Treaty, signed between the US (by President Reagan) and USSR (by Premier Gorbachev) in 1987, agreed the removal of missiles from Greenham, with the final warheads being removed in 1991.

In its heyday, the airbase was virtually a self-contained American city, with everything from baseball pitches to its own school. The 1,000-acre (405ha) site even hosted international air shows, and some local people feared that it might become the new London airport. Today, thanks to a multi-million pound redevelopment, Greenham Common is being restored to its pre-World War II state. Its open, windswept landscape is dramatically different from the sheltered walking beside the Kennet and Avon Canal and the River Lambourn.

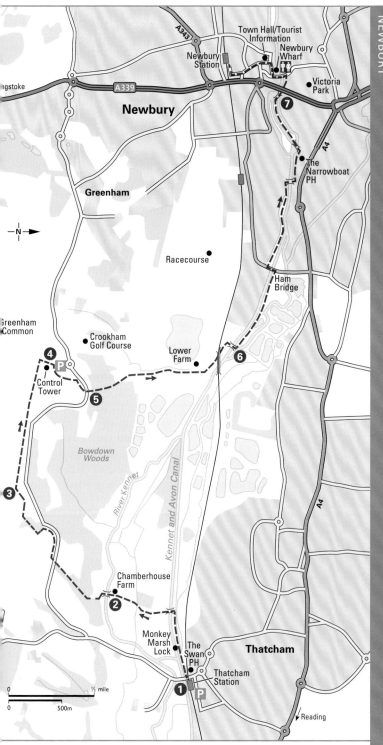

Town Hall/Tourist Information

Newbury Wharf

Newbury Station

Victoria Park

A343

A339

ngstoke

Newbury

Greenham

The Narrowboat PH

A4

—N→

Greenham Common

Racecourse

Ham Bridge

Crookham Golf Course

Lower Farm

6

4

P

Control Tower

5

Bowdown Woods

River Kennet

Kennet and Avon Canal

A4

3

Chamberhouse Farm

2

Monkey Marsh Lock

The Swan PH

Thatcham

Thatcham Station

1

P

↓ Reading

0 ───── ½ mile

0 ───── 500m

1 From the station, cross the road and join the canal towards Ham Bridge. Pass Monkey Marsh Lock – unusual in that it is turf-sided – and at the swing bridge turn left towards Chamberhouse Farm. Pass between the outbuildings and follow the drive past the farmhouse and cottages.

2 Cross the river, and just beyond it the drive curves left. Keep right here and follow the track as it runs steeply up through woodland to the road. Cross over to a gate leading onto Crookham Common and turn right. Follow the path parallel to the road. Walk on and follow the stony path which winds to join the long, straight former military taxi-way.

3 The old control tower comes into view and you pass a log carved to make seats. Continue past a copse, and when the tower reappears, branch off right and go through a gate past the tower, leaving the Common.

4 Turn right in front of the car park. After around 20 paces turn sharp left along a hedge (with the car park, left), past a rusted boiler, to a field gate and walker's gate which takes you (briefly) back onto the Common. Continue and soon pass through another gate. Keep to the left of the field, and beyond the fence corner, at a small waymarker post pointing straight ahead, bear left. Go through the gap in the hedge, then left to a wire fence, then right, and after 40 paces go left through a

gate. Descend to the road bend, cross it (carefully) and head down through trees into Bowdown Woods.

5 Pass Bowdown Farm and on your left is a golf course. To left and right are disused quarry workings. Continue on the lane to a stile and gate; go over and keep ahead, passing beside Lower Farm and Newbury Racecourse. Veer left under the railway, and reach a swing bridge, right, over the canal.

6 Cross the canal, turn left and follow the tow path to Ham Bridge. Go up and across the bridge, then turn right to follow the path along the south bank. Continue on a leafy stretch of tow path past Newbury Boat Company moorings, then cross over the canal again at the next footbridge, with Tesco's and The Narrow Boat pub on the north bank. Keep to the path and cross the next bridge at the entrance to a marina. Pass picturesque Greenham Lock.

7 Go under the road through a gate and alongside Victoria Park before reaching the next bridge. Leave the tow path and cross the canal into what was Newbury Wharf, then keep right past the West Berkshire Museum and continue ahead. Turn left in the Market Place and follow Cheap Street. At its right-hand bend, continue ahead, passing the Baptist Church, then go round to the right for Newbury Station and the train back to Thatcham.

WHERE TO EAT AND DRINK The Swan in Thatcham is an attractive pub at the start/finish of the walk. En route is The Narrow Boat, close to the canal. Alternatively, continue on a little further to Newbury town centre where there is an excellent range of pubs, cafes, bars and restaurants.

WHAT TO SEE The 'churring' song of the nightjar has replaced the roar of aero engines at Greenham Common. Listen out, too, for the Dartford warbler and the woodlark, among Britain's rarest birds.

On John Betjeman's trail at Farnborough

DISTANCE 7.5 miles (12.1km) MINIMUM TIME 3hrs

ASCENT/GRADIENT 150ft (46m) ▲▲▲ LEVEL OF DIFFICULTY +++

PATHS Bridleways, field paths, tracks and quiet lanes

LANDSCAPE Remote downland country to south of the Ridgeway

SUGGESTED MAP OS Explorer 170 Abingdon & Wantage

START/FINISH Grid reference: SU471825

DOG FRIENDLINESS Under control across farmland

PARKING Room to park in West Ilsley's main street

PUBLIC TOILETS None on route

John Betjeman (1906-84) has been described as the most popular poet of the 20th century. With his infectious laugh, air of eccentricity and sense of fun, he was an immensely popular character, and having been born into the television age, he was a natural performer for that particular medium. He loved the camera and it loved him in return.

HOME ON THE DOWNS

Over the years Betjeman has been the subject of many distinguished television documentaries which demonstrated his love for architecture, for historic landmarks and endangered buildings, showing how he brought them to life in his own highly individual style.

However, few of these TV biographies make any mention of his home in the splendid, rambling Old Rectory in the tiny Berkshire village of Farnborough. Betjeman and his wife Penelope moved here in 1945. Betjeman spent World War II as a press attaché in Dublin, and when it was finally over, he and Penelope returned to their beloved Berkshire. He worked mainly in London, mixing with writers, poets and Oxbridge intellectuals. But he was most at home in the peace and tranquillity of the countryside – especially the Vale of the White Horse, then still within Berkshire. Betjeman loved to explore the downs on foot, while Penelope galloped along the Ridgeway on Moti, her Arab mare.

AN INSPIRATION

During the six years he lived in Farnborough, Betjeman was typically productive in his work output. His collection of verse, *New Bats in Old Belfries*, was published in 1945, and in 1948 his *Selected Poems* won the Heinemann Award for Literature. He also worked on Murray's *Architectural Guide for Berkshire*, published in 1949.

The Betjemans moved to Wantage in 1951. It wasn't far away, and here the poet continued to indulge his love of the English countryside. In a TV interview in 1984, the year he died, Betjeman said that 'poetry makes life worth living', believing that the greatest thing he had done in his own life was to use his eyes and his feelings.

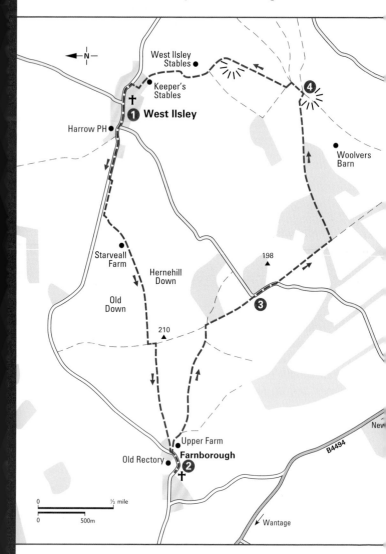

1 Follow the road west out of West Ilsley, passing the village signs. At the first gap in the hedge walk on the footpath parallel to the road. Take the first bridleway on the left and follow the track past Starveall Farm uphill to a gate. Continue ahead, with the field boundary on your right. Bear left through a gate at the next junction onto an ancient track. Soon bear right, passing a broken stile, to follow the path across a large field. Go straight ahead at the waymarked corner and keep ahead in the next field, with the

fence on your right. Follow the path across the field to the road, passing a water tower. By Upper Farm veer left and go past the Old Rectory, to your right, and continue along the road to Farnborough Church (on the left, at the bend).

2 Walk back along the road to the farm, rejoin the track beside the outbuildings and look for a waymarker and a pair of galvanised gates after about 60yds (55m). A field footpath and two tracks can be seen here. Keep right, directly beside the farm. Cut between trees, bushes and margins of vegetation and soon cross a footpath junction. Go further on between dense hedges. Continue ahead to a junction with a byway and bridleway. Keep ahead, going through woodland, following the Ilsley Downs Riding Route. Make for the next junction, where you can see a field beyond the trees – bear right and follow the clear path through the woods.

3 Keep right at the road, and when it bends right, go straight on along a bridleway running across the fields towards trees. The bridleway

eventually becomes a byway. Keep ahead when you reach a bend and walk along to a waymarked track on the left. Follow it into the woodland and down the slope. As you approach a gap in the hedge, with a field seen ahead, veer right to follow a path running through the trees. Eventually it climbs gently to a junction. The walk turns left, but it is worth stepping to your right for several paces to admire the timeless view of Woolvers Barn and Woolvers Down.

4 Follow the byway, avoiding the public footpath on your right, and take the next bridleway on the left. Keep right at the next junction and cut between hedges. When the track bends left, there is a memorable view of West Ilsley sitting snugly in its downland setting. Keep right at the next junction, following the track alongside West Ilsley Stables. Cross a cattle grid and turn left along the drive. Walk down to the road and turn left. As it bends right by a bridleway sign, go straight on by Keeper's Stables. Swing left as you reach the centre of West Ilsley and pass All Saints Church to return to the start.

WHERE TO EAT AND DRINK Overlooking the cricket ground in West Ilsley, the Harrow is a charming village pub. Inside is an appealing open-plan bar offering quality food and imaginatively prepared dishes.

WHAT TO SEE Although the Old Rectory House is never open to the public, its beautiful 4-acre (1.6ha) garden, created more than 30 years ago, is open on a few summer Sundays via the National Gardens Scheme, and may also be visited by pre-booked groups. Those few lucky visitors who do attend can enjoy a series of immaculately tended garden rooms, including herbaceous borders, an arboretum, a 'boule-a-drome', roses and clematis, vegetable gardens, and magnificent views.

WHILE YOU'RE THERE Make a point of looking at the west window in Farnborough's All Saints Church, dedicated to the memory of John Betjeman. The window, which depicts the tree of life, was designed by Betjeman's friend John Piper and executed by Joseph Nuttgens. Have a look at West Ilsley, noted for its horse-racing connections and pretty cottages. Opposite the pub is a striking gazebo, erected by the villagers to mark the new Millennium. Look out, too, for the attractively designed parish paths map.

Around Chaddleworth

DISTANCE 5.75 miles (9.2km)   MINIMUM TIME 2hrs 15min

ASCENT/GRADIENT 269ft (82m) ▲▲▲   LEVEL OF DIFFICULTY ✦✦✦

PATHS Field paths and tracks, stretches of road; many stiles

LANDSCAPE Classic farmland and remote, rolling country on edge of Lambourn Downs

SUGGESTED MAP OS Explorer 158 Newbury & Hungerford

START/FINISH Grid reference: SU415772

DOG FRIENDLINESS On lead near livestock and in region of Whatcombe

PARKING Public car park by The Ibex pub

PUBLIC TOILETS None on route

The sweeping Lambourn Downs lie at the heart of Berkshire's loveliest and most isolated country – an area with a long tradition for racehorse training. Whatcombe racing stables and stud (passed on this walk) is nationally famous, and several Derby winners have been trained on nearby Woolley Downs, one of the best training gallops in the country, known for the superb quality of its turf.

THE SPORT OF KINGS

Horse racing dates back to the days of chariot races in Greece and Rome, with blockbuster movies like the immortal *Ben-Hur* (1958) giving us a flavour of what it would have been like to vie for honours in the ancient arenas. Racing as we know it today has its origins in the period of the Stuart kings. James I established stables at Newmarket, in Suffolk, and it was here that he kept racehorses and 'riders for the races' – the first royal jockeys.

Towards the end of the 17th century racehorses were beginning to appear all over the country, with many breeders introducing Arabian stock. Three of these stallions were the sires from which all our thoroughbreds are descended. As the sport began to draw spectator interest, it split into two categories: flat racing and racing over jumps.

DOWNS FOR GALLOPS

Training stables were soon a permanent feature of life in the countryside, but they had to have easy access to large tracts of open downland and grassland over which gallops could be laid for racing practice. As the flinty, chalk soil made this landscape unsuitable for ploughing, the Lambourn Downs were considered ideal terrain for horses to compete with one another and jockeys to sharpen and hone their skills.

Before the 1840s horses were treated with little care or compassion. They were taken on long gallops and wrapped in thick rugs to make them sweat. More suitable methods of training were introduced, which enabled trainers to look at each horse individually and assess its potential, fitness level and merit as a future winner.

Take a walk on the Lambourn Downs and you'll find it's not just horses and their jockeys who frequent this breezy corner of Berkshire – walkers love it, too. Yet often you can go there and be completely alone. Other than occasional birdsong and the rustle of trees sighing gently in the breeze, there is not a sound to be heard.

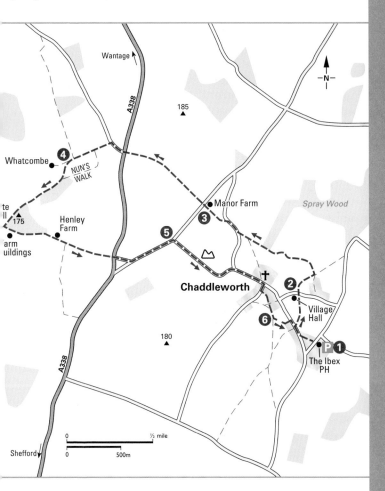

❶ From The Ibex take the path opposite the pub, emerging at the next road by three thatched cottages. Keep right and follow the lane for 100yds (91m) to some steps and a footpath on the right. Follow the grassy path which cuts between fields, towards houses. Keep to the right of

the village hall and cross the road to a kissing gate.

❷ Skirt the field, ignore a footpath on the left and continue straight ahead. Bear right and go through two gates in quick succession, and keep a horse paddock on your left.

Turn left at the end of the paddock (so it still to your left) and keep along the field-edge. Eventually the path begins to descend steeply, with Manor Farm visible below to the right, and becomes a track. Go over a stile and straight on at the road. Just before it bends right, look for a waymarked track on the left, descending to Manor Farm.

3 Cross the road and follow the path up the slope to a stile. Continue straight ahead, through the gap to the left of the roped-off posts, between wire fences, and ascend the steep slope to the brow of the hill. Descend the slope (the path may be overgrown) to the corner of the field, climbing over a small section of fencing, with two stiles adjacent. Go over these and make the sharp descent straight ahead downhill. The gallops at Whatcombe are clearly visible across the fields below. Cross a stile, then another to reach the road. Follow the sign to Whatcombe and South Fawley. Turn left at the entrance to the Whatcombe Estate and go through the gate. On reaching the Stud, keep left and take the waymarked bridleway.

4 Climb gradually, and where the track bears left continue ahead on a grassy path. Veer left to a gap in the corner of the field, leading to a small wood. Soon through the wood, the path continues to the left, along its edge. Descend the bank to the overgrown path at the corner of the field and turn left, down onto a path by an electricity generator and mobile phone mast. After a few paces emerge from the trees and fork left onto a track, continuing downhill with farm outbuildings to your right. Pass the attractive buildings of Henley Farm and follow the byway down to the road. Cross to a narrow lane and bear left at the next junction.

5 Take the first narrow, unmarked lane on the right and climb steeply to a left-hand bend. Walk along to the next junction, turn right and pass the village sign for Chaddleworth. The church is on the left. Turn right towards Shefford, and take the first path left. Enter a field via a squeeze stile and cross it, keeping to the left-hand boundary and passing a large house.

6 Cross another squeeze stile, in the corner, and go left around the field-edge after a few paces, at a public footpath sign wreathed in nettles and foliage. After another 50 or so paces turn left and drop down to a modern housing development. Turn right at the main road and retrace your steps back to The Ibex, veering left along the path after the third thatched cottage.

WHERE TO EAT AND DRINK The only source of refreshments along the route is The Ibex at Chaddleworth. Formerly a cosy award-winning pub and village post office combined, it's future is currently uncertain, so check ahead.

WHAT TO SEE As you walk through Whatcombe Estate, look for the striking bronze statue of Snurge who won the St Ledger in 1990. Whatcombe has produced several Classics winners over the years.

WHILE YOU'RE THERE St Andrew's Church, Chaddleworth, welcomes visitors with a fine carved Norman doorway and a Norman nave. It houses a fine collection of Georgian and Victorian memorials. Its oldest monument (dated 1619), above the pulpit, is dedicated to Elisabeth and Dorothy Nelson.

From Inkpen to Combe Gibbet

DISTANCE 8.5 miles (13.7km)	**MINIMUM TIME** 4hrs
ASCENT/GRADIENT 725ft (221m) ▲▲▲	**LEVEL OF DIFFICULTY** +++

PATHS Woodland paths, field and downland tracks, some road walking; several stiles

LANDSCAPE Gentle farmland, steep scarp of Inkpen Hill and lofty heights of Wessex downs

SUGGESTED MAP OS Explorer 158 Newbury & Hungerford

START/FINISH Grid reference: SU378639

DOG FRIENDLINESS Signs at intervals request dogs on leads

PARKING On public byway beside Crown and Garter, Inkpen Common

PUBLIC TOILETS None on route

Stand at the foot of Inkpen Hill on a bleak winter's afternoon and look for the outline of Combe Gibbet, just visible against the darkening sky. This has to be one of the wildest, most dramatic scenes in southern England. These lonely Wessex downs have a timeless quality to them.

CRIME SCENE

The gibbet doesn't look much close up – but one has stood here for almost 350 years. The original gibbet was erected in 1676 following the conviction of a local labourer, George Broomham, and his mistress Dorothy Newman. The pair's plans to be together were complicated by Broomham's wife Martha and his young son Robert. They resorted to drastic measures, lying in wait for the boy and his mother on the crest of the hill. Eventually Martha and Robert appeared, out for a walk on the downs. Broomham and Newman sprang an ambush, clubbing them to death with cudgels. It was a most vicious double murder – savage and ultimately pointless.

The murderers were caught and appeared at Winchester Assizes in February, 1676, where they were found guilty. It was decreed that they should be 'hanged in chaynes near the place of the murder'. The execution took place in March, and it is said that the bodies could be seen hanging from several counties. Vandalism and the elements call for a new gibbet every so often, but successive structures over the years have ensured that the memory of that dreadful incident is kept alive.

The gruesome events of that winter so long ago became the subject of a film, made in the late 1940s. Written and directed by Alan Cooke and John Schlesinger, who was then making his debut as a film director, *The Black Legend* captured the sense of isolation conveyed by this part of Berkshire, and a local cast reinforced the realism.

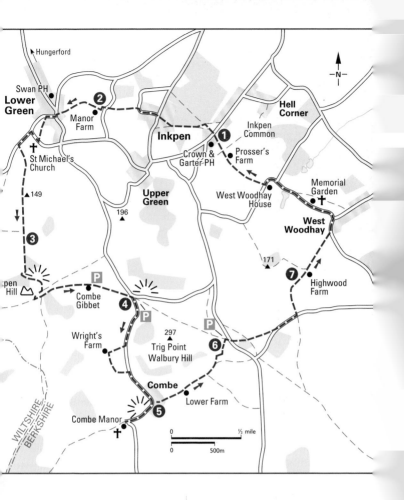

1 Cross over the road from the Crown and Garter pub and follow the waymarked track, passing the entrance to the thatched cottage opposite the pub. Keep right at the first fork, then almost immediately fork left. Follow the woodland trail to a junction of paths by an old marker stone and swing left. Keep to the path, skirting the woods. Emerge from the trees, pass Mistletoe Cottage and turn right at the first kissing gate. Follow the path over the field to a kissing gate. Cross the road to a lane and follow it; this becomes a track and heads round to the right. Go through a gate, left, and descend two steps between wire fences to two kissing

gates. Cross the field towards Manor Farm and go through a kissing gate, across the lane.

2 Follow a path between fences to the right of Manor Farm. Continue on this path, then bear left at the opening. After a few paces go through a kissing gate and follow sections of boardwalk. Cross a footbridge, pass a tree house on the right, then go alongside a beech hedge to the road. Bear left, signed 'Ham and Shalbourne'. After Westcourt Cottage turn left to a gate, then cross a stile and follow the fence. Cross into the next field via a stile, towards Inkpen Church and another stile. Go over

Left: Combe Gibbet stands high on Inkpen Beacon (Walk 49)

this, turn right down to the junction. Bear left, pass village sign, and swing left to follow a waymarked track. Continue through the metal gate to the next waymarker, then keep a line of trees and bushes on the right before heading out across open fields. Make for the next waymarker and keep ahead between the trees.

③ The path climbs gradually to a gate and waymarker. Go through the gate then start ascending steeply, diagonally left. As the path reaches the summit and bends left, look straight ahead for a gate in the field boundary. Go through here, aiming for a metal gate ahead, and turn left to join a byway. Follow the track to Combe Gibbet. Continue down the track to the road.

④ At the road turn right, downhill. Turn right at the entrance to Wright's Farm and continue to the farmhouse and outbuildings. Bear left at the waymarker and follow the track as it curves back to the road. Turn right to the village of Combe. With the village houses to your left, make a detour, continuing to follow the road round to the right. After a few paces ascend a path on the left that runs beside the road. The road switches back sharply on itself at the entrance to Combe Manor. To the left of this a drive leads to St Swithun's Church, hidden to the left. To the right of the entrance to the house is a field with a view of the gibbet against the skyline. Walbury Hill (974ft/297m), Britain's highest chalk summit, can be seen from here. Return to the centre of the hamlet.

⑤ Turn right, signed to Lower Farm. Pass a footpath on the right and keep ahead on the track. On reaching the buildings of Lower Farm, follow the waymarked byway; the track climbs steadily between trees. At a right-hand bend, look for a public bridleway sign and veer left off the track, passing through a gate. Follow the bridleway to a fork and veer left to join a sunken path. To your left the buildings of Combe can be seen below. Continue to the next fork and keep right. The path now disappears. Climb up above clumps of gorse, go left of a small tree and keep ascending. At the top boundary of the field, over towards the left (but not in the very corner), look for a stile. Cross onto the track, turn right and head downhill.

⑥ Cross the road to a gate and head diagonally left down the field, towards the left-hand corner of the copse ahead. Follow the path as it veers to the left of the woodland, making for a gate in the fence. Go through and walk down the lane for 200yds (183m), then turn left at the bridleway sign. Follow the path straight ahead between fields, sweeping right to pass Highwood Farm.

⑦ Join a concrete track and follow it, left, to the road. Turn left, keep left at the next junction and pass St Laurence's Church. Pass West Woodhay House and a turning for Kintbury, and follow the road round a left bend. Turn right 80yds (73m) beyond it at a restricted byway sign. Continue straight on past Prosser's Farm to return to the start.

WHERE TO EAT AND DRINK The Swan at Lower Green is one of West Berkshire's most popular pubs, offering well-presented dishes. Next door is a shop selling organic produce where you can stock up before leaving. The Crown and Garter at Inkpen Common is also popular and serves a good range of food and drink.

By the Kennet and Avon Canal at Enborne

DISTANCE 4 miles (6.4km)   MINIMUM TIME 1hr 30min

ASCENT/GRADIENT 90ft (27m) ▲▲▲   LEVEL OF DIFFICULTY ✚✚✚

PATHS Tracks, roads, estate drives and canal tow path

LANDSCAPE Lowland country bisected by the canal; elegant parkland on south side of Kennet Valley

SUGGESTED MAP OS Explorer 158 Newbury & Hungerford

START/FINISH Grid reference: SU435657

DOG FRIENDLINESS Under control on canal tow path; lead required in Hamstead Park

PARKING Car park by Enborne Church

PUBLIC TOILETS None on route

Completed in 1810, the 87-mile (140km) long Kennet and Avon Canal took 16 years to construct. The final bill was in the region of £1 million. With 104 locks and many other impressive features, the canal was regarded as a triumph of engineering.

The Kennet and Avon was built to provide a direct trade link between London and Bristol, thus avoiding the treacherous south coast route which took ships around Land's End. The canal eventually became redundant in the late 1940s, but dedicated armies of supporters were determined not to let it die. Restored over many years, the canal was eventually re-opened by the Queen at Devizes in 1990. Since then it has become one of southern England's most colourful and vibrant waterways.

DRAWING THE LINE

But 60 years ago, it would have been a very different story. Follow the canal tow path and you'll spot ugly brick and concrete pill boxes at intervals along the bank. Unsightly though they undoubtedly are, they are vivid reminders of World War II and the time when Britain braced itself for invasion. Cutting a swathe across England from east to west, the waterway was to act as the second line of defence if the Germans had breached the south coast blockade. In fact more than 50 defensive lines were constructed around Britain, the longest and most important being the GHQ (General Head Quarters Line) designed to protect London and the industrial heart of Britain. This ran from Somerset along the River Brue and the Kennet and Avon Canal to Reading, and the pill boxes you pass on this walk are part of that network. Tank traps were laid to deter the enemy from making deeper inroads, and concrete machine gun posts were also positioned along the tow path to guard the open, undefended country to the south.

As history tells us, none of these defences ever had to be tested, and the most recent warfare that this peaceful part of the world has experienced remains over 370 years distant. This occurred during the Civil War in 1643, when Parliamentary troops were stationed in Hamstead Marshall Park for the first Battle of Newbury, part of which was fought at neighbouring Wash Common. During their stay it is recorded that they ruined the house that preceded the Earl of Craven's grand mansion there.

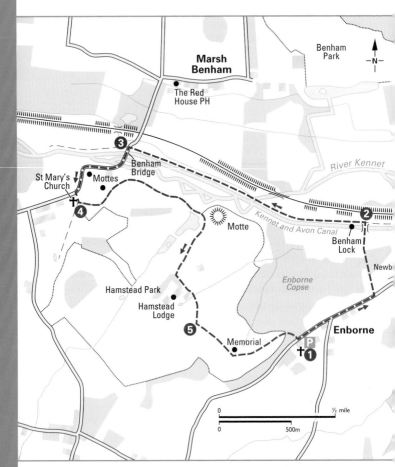

❶ From the car park turn right onto the road towards Newbury. Pass Church Lane, and as the road descends the buildings of Newbury edge into view. Take the next signposted footpath left, at the entrance to Step Up Cottage,

and continue straight on along the track. Follow it across open fields and through a kissing gate; soon the Kennet and Avon Canal comes into view ahead. Once over the bridge, turn left by a pill box and go down to the tow path.

② Continue heading west, past Benham Lock and then a tributary stream running into some woods. The railway line is seen on the right along this stretch. A little further on, at Benham Broad, the river and canal unite.

③ Leave the tow path and cross the river by the old brick Benham Bridge, then cross another (level) bridge and pass Hamstead Mill, formerly belonging to the Craven Estate. Continue on the road beside a brick wall. Where the road curves right, continue ahead on a footpath leading to St Mary's Church, Hamstead Marshall. With the back of the church in front of you, to your left, in the corner of the churchyard is the mausoleum containing the Craven family vault. Take the gate, left, leading out to parkland, with two sets of large gate piers to the right. This is Hamstead Park (also known as Hamstead Marshall Park).

④ Follow the grassy track as it bends left and descends between trees to a drive. Turn right, following it through a landscape dotted with ancient oak and gnarled beech trees. After a while,

pass over a cattle grid and enjoy the most picturesque part of this walk, with languid grassy ponds and an ornamental bridge below. Follow the drive until you leave this bucolic scene behind, then after a left-hand bend, go past a turning on the left. As the drive sweeps right towards a gate and cream-coloured houses, go straight on along a path, over a small footbridge and through a kissing gate, to an avenue of horse chestnut trees. On the right is Hamstead Lodge (also called Hamstead Park), former home of the Craven family, and one of the lodges of the great mansion that burned down. After the Cravens departed, it became a nursing home and is now a private residence.

⑤ Turn left and follow the drive, passing a large stone dedicated to the men of the American Parachute Regiment. In 1944 they prepared here for the D-Day Landings, and returned briefly to Hamstead before departing to parachute into Holland on 7 September, in the battle to liberate Europe. Follow the drive to the exit (with cattle grid), and opposite is the car park where the walk began.

WHERE TO EAT AND DRINK A five-minute walk from the main route (usually signposted with a blackboard on the tow path at Benham Bridge) lies The Red House at Marsh Benham, a picturesque thatched dining pub owned by a French chef. The food is high quality, the beer is good, there is an attractive garden and they even offer afternoon tea.

WHAT TO SEE Sir William Craven built a magnificent mansion at Hamstead Park in 1660, but the house was destroyed by fire and all that remains of it in situ are the eight pairs of elaborate gateposts, some now crumbling and overgrown, evocative of grand Classical ruins. The house was designed by the eminent Anglo-Dutch architect, Sir Balthazar Gerbier.

WHILE YOU'RE THERE The 12th-century church at Enborne, dedicated to St Michael and All Angels, is notable for its Saxon font decorated with emblems of the Passion; a fresco painted by an Italian monk from Sandleford Priory; and a bell cast in 1260. Unfortunately the church is usually only open for services, so make prior arrangements if you wish to visit.

Titles in the series